60 seconds to
shine.

MONOLOGUES FOR MEN

60 SECONDS TO

Shine

VOLUME 1

221 ONE-MINUTE MONOLOGUES FOR MEN

EDITED BY
JOHN CAPECCI AND
IRENE ZIEGLER ASTON

MONOLOGUE AUDITION SERIES

A Smith and Kraus Book

Published by Smith and Kraus, Inc.
177 Lyme Road, Hanover, NH 03755
www.SmithandKraus.com

First Edition: April 2006
6 5 4 3 2 1

Cover and text design by Julia Hill Gignoux
Manufactured in the United States of America

The Monologue Audition Series   ISSN 1067-134X

Library of Congress Cataloguing-in-Publication Data
60 seconds to shine. Volume 1, 221 one-minute monologues for men / edited by John Capecci and Irene Ziegler Aston.-- 1st ed.
    p. cm. -- (Monologue audition series, ISSN 1067-134X)
  ISBN-10 1-57525-400-X ISBN-13 978-1-57525-400-5
  1. Monologues. 2. Acting--Auditions. 3. Men--Drama. I. Title: Sixty seconds to shine. II. Title: 221 one-minute monologues for men. III. Title: Two hundred and twenty one one-minute monologues for men. IV. Title: Two hundred twenty one one-minute monologues for men. V. Capecci, John. VI. Aston, Irene Ziegler, 1955- VII. Series.

PN2080.A1225 2006
808.82'45089286--dc22

                                                                    2006042304

NOTE: These monologues are intended to be used for audition and class study; permission is not required to use the material for those purposes. However, if there is a paid performance of any of the monologues included in this book, please contact the publisher for permission information.

TABLE OF CONTENTS

CLASSICAL MONOLOGUES

CONTEMPORARY MONOLOGUES

INTRODUCTION

Upon learning of today's typical cattle-call audition process, Dustin Hoffman—who hasn't had to audition in a long, long time—once declared that if he had only a minute to make an impression, he'd take off his clothes. For those of us who would rather think inside the box, here are two hundred and twenty-one monologues, all one minute or under in performance length.

For those auditions or class assignments where brevity is crucial, you need a monologue that gets to the point. You need a defined character, strong emotional content, and a resonant ending. Just as important, you need a lot of monologues from which to choose. This book offers you that, and more.

In our continuing effort to offer you new sources of monologues, we've drawn from plays, novels, short stories, poems, original monologues, essays, comics, novellas, radio plays, film scripts, and personal narratives.

How to Use This Book. At the back of this volume, you'll find all 221 monologues indexed according to *age, tone,* and *voice*, to help identify those most suited to your needs:

Age is noted exactly only when specified by the author. More often, we've indicated an age range (20s, 20s-30s). In some instances, we've used a plus sign to show the character could be older than indicated, as in 40+.

Classic/Contemporary refers to when the monologue was written, not necessarily when the character is speaking.

"Classic" texts are those that were written prior to the early 1920s.

Voice refers to indications of class, geography, ethnicity, nationality, sexual identity, or physicality that may help performers gain entry into an individual character, or closely "match" themselves to a monologue. The language of any text will reveal a certain level of education, class, or knowledge. Sometimes, however, a monologue arises out of specific cultural experience, demonstrated either through content or language. Those are the selections you'll find listed in the "Voice" index.

Whenever possible, we've attempted to excerpt monologues with a minimum of editing. Where editing was necessary, omissions are indicated by parenthetical ellipses (. . .). All other ellipses were part of the original text.

We offer appropriately brief contexts to help you gain some entry into the monologues. But, of course, in order to fully understand and ultimately embody the characters, you are strongly advised to read the play, novel, poem, etc. from which the monologue was drawn. The greater context must be fully explored in order to answer the all-important questions: who, what, when, where, why.

So—go forth and be brief. Just keep your shirt on.

ACKNOWLEDGMENTS

The editors are grateful to a number of people for assistance with these one-minute monologue books as well as the two-minute monologue books, in which we shamefully forgot to say thanks. Here then, is a double dose of appreciation to those who deserve much more:

Marisa Smith, Eric Kraus, and their staff, for taking us on.

The Department of Theatre and Dance, the University of Richmond, for the generous use of its excellent drama library.

D.L. Lepidus, for persisting in a thankless job.

Laurie Walker, for contributions and support.

All our smart and funny friends, who pointed us to their favorite monologues.

Graham and Rob, who get us.

Google™, which has changed our lives.

CLASSICAL
MONOLOGUES

The Affairs of Anatol
Arthur Schnitzler
Translation by Marya Mannes

Play
35+
Dramatic

Anatol, who has a habit of "rescuing" women, laments the fleeting nature of infatuations.

There really isn't any more to it. I had known her only two hours and I knew that I would probably never see her again once the evening was over—she told me so herself—and yet I had the feeling that I was loved madly in that moment. It wrapped me round—the air was heavy and fragrant with this love—do you understand? And again I had the foolish and divine thought—"you poor, poor child." The episodic character of it all came so clearly to my consciousness. While I still felt her warm breath on my hand, I seemed to be living it over in my memory—as if it were already a thing of the past. She was just another one of those over whom my path led me. The word came to me then—that arid word "Episode"—and yet I seemed to feel myself as something Eternal. I knew that this poor child would never lose the memory of this hour—I had never felt so sure of it as in just this case. Oh, I often realize that by next morning I will be quite forgotten. But this was different—I was all the world to this girl who lay at my feet—I felt the sacred, enduring love with which she surrounded me— one can feel that—I know that in that moment she had thought for nothing but me—and yet for me she was already something that was past—something that was fleeting—an Episode.

Antony and Cleopatra
William Shakespeare

30s+
Dramatic

Antony feels duped by Cleopatra.

All is lost!
This foul Egyptian hath betrayed me:
My fleet hath yielded to the foe, and yonder
They cast their caps up and carouse together
Like friends long lost. Triple-turned whore! 'tis thou
Has sold me to this novice, and my heart
Makes only wars on thee. Bid them all fly;
For when I am revenged upon my charm,
I have done all. Bid them all fly, begone.
O sun, thy uprise shall I see no more.
Fortune and Antony part here, even here
Do we shake hands. All come to this? The hearts
That spanieled me at heels, to whom I gave
Their wishes, do discandy, melt their sweets
On blossoming Caesar; and this pine is barked,
That overtopped them all. Betrayed I am.
O this false soul of Egypt! this grave charm,
Whose eye becked forth my wars, and called them home,
Whose bosom was my crownet, my chief end,
Like a right gypsy hath at fast and loose
Beguiled me to the very heart of loss.
What, Eros, Eros!

Antony and Cleopatra

William Shakespeare

Play
30s+
Dramatic

Antony confronts Cleopatra, who has betrayed him.

What, Eros, Eros! *(Enter CLEOPATRA.)* Ah, thou spell!
    Avaunt!
Vanish, or I shall give thee thy deserving
And blemish Caesar's triumph. Let him take thee
And hoist thee up to the shouting plebeians;
Follow his chariot, like the greatest spot
Of all thy sex. Most monster-like be shown
For poor'st diminitives, for dolts, and let
Patient Octavia plough thy visage up
With her preparèd nails. *(Exit CLEOPATRA.)* 'Tis well th' art
    gone,
If it be well to live; but better 'twere
Thou fell'st into my fury, for one death
Might have prevented many. Eros, ho!
The shirt of Nessus is upon me; teach me,
Alcides, thou mine ancestor, thy rage.
Let me lodge Lichas on the horns o' th' moon
And with those hands that grasped the heaviest club
Subdue my worthiest self. The witch shall die.
To the young Roman boy she hath sold me, and I fall
Under his plot: she dies for 't. Eros, ho!

The Beaver Coat

Gerhart Hauptmann

Translated by Ludwig Lewisohn

Play
40+
Comic

Mitteldorf warns Mrs. Wolff of trouble brewing.

He's writin' pages an' pages! An' them must be important things, I c'n tell you that. *(Confidentially.)* An' lemme tell you: there's somethin' in the air—I ain't sayin' I know exactly what. But there's somethin'—I know that as sure's . . . You just look out, that's all, and you'll live to see it. It's goin' to come down—somethin'—and when it do—look out. That's all I say. No, I don't pretend to understand them things. It's all new doin's to me. That's what they calls modern. An' I don't know nothin' about that. But somethin's got to happen. Things can't go on this way. The whole place is got to be cleaned out. I can't say's I gets the hang of it. I'm too old. But talk about the justice what died. Why, he wasn't nothin' but a dam' fool to this one. I could go an' tell you all kinds o' things, but I ain't got no time. The baron'll be missin' me. *(He goes, but having arrived at the door, turns back.)* The lightnin' is goin' to strike, Mrs. Wolff. Take my word for that!

Before Dawn

Gerhart Hauptmann

Translated by Ludwig Lewisohn

Play
30+
Dramatic

Hoffmann, an engineer, dissuades a young upstart from revealing working conditions in the coal mines.

I must tell you that I consider your appearance and demeanor here—to put it mildly—incredibly impudent. You come here, enjoy my hospitality, thresh out a few of your thread-bare phrases, turn my sister-in-law's head, go on about old friendships and other pleasant things, and then you tell me quite coolly: you're going to write a descriptive pamphlet about the local conditions. Why, what do you take me to be, anyhow? D'you suppose I don't know that these so-called essays are merely shameless libels? . . . You want to write a denunciation like that, and about our coal district, of all places! Are you so blind that you can't see whom such a rag would harm most keenly? Only me, of course! I tell you, the trade that you demagogues drive ought to be more firmly stamped out than has been done up to now! What is it you do? You make the miners discontent, presumptuous; you stir them up, embitter them, make them rebellious, disobedient, wretched! Then you delude them with promises of mountains of gold, and, in the meantime, grab out of their pockets the few pennies that keep them from starving! You ridiculous, pompous wind-bag! Go to work! Leave off this silly driveling! Do something!

The Blunderer
Molière
Translated by Henri van Laun

Play
20+
Comic

Mascarille informs his friend that his infatuation with a certain young woman has not gone unnoticed.

Your love is like porridge, which by too fierce a fire swells, mounts up to the brim, and runs over everywhere! Everybody might have seen it. At table, when Trufaldin made her sit down, you never took your eyes off her, blushed, looked quite silly, cast sheep's eyes at her, without ever minding what you were helped to; you were never thirsty but when she drank, and took the glass eagerly from her hands; and without rinsing it, or throwing a drop if it away, you drank what she left in it, and seemed to choose in preference that side of the glass which her lips had touched; upon every piece which her slender hand had touched, or which she had bit, you laid your paw as quickly as a cat does upon a mouse, and you swallowed it as glibly as if you were a regular glutton. Then, besides all this, you made an intolerable noise, shuffling with your feet under the table, for which Trufaldin, who received two lusty kicks, twice punished a couple of innocent dogs, who would have growled at you if they dared; and yet, in spite of all this, you say you have behaved finely! For my part I sat upon thorns all the time; notwithstanding the cold, I feel even now in a perspiration. I hung over you just as a bowler does over his ball after he has thrown it, and thought to restrain your actions by contorting my body ever so many times!

The Boor

Anton Chekhov
Translated by Mason W. Cartwright
Play
30+
Comic

Smirnov swears off women.

I don't understand how to behave in the company of ladies. Madam, in the course of my life I have seen more women than you have sparrows. Three times have I fought duels for women, twelve I jilted and nine jilted me. There was a time when I played the fool, used honeyed language, bowed and scraped. I loved, suffered, sighed to the moon, melted in love's torments. I loved passionately, I loved to madness, loved in every key, chattered like a magpie on emancipation, sacrificed half my fortune in the tender passion, until now the devil knows I've had enough of it. Your obedient servant will let you lead him around by the nose no more. Enough! Black eyes, passionate eyes, coral lips, dimples in cheeks, moonlight whispers, soft, modest sights—for all that, madam, I wouldn't pay a kopeck! I am not speaking of present company, but of women in general; from the tiniest to the greatest, they are conceited, hypocritical, chattering, odious, deceitful from top to toe; vain, petty, cruel with a maddening logic and in this respect, please excuse my frankness, but one sparrow is worth ten of the aforementioned petticoat-philosophers.

The Castle Spectre

Matthew G. Lewis

Translated by Henri van Laun

Play
50s
Dramatic

Reginald, a man held captive for sixteen years by his evil brother, wakes from a dream about his daughter.

My child! My Evelina!—Oh! fly me not, lovely forms!—They arc gone, and once more I live to misery—Thou wert kind to me, Sleep!—Even now, methought, "I sat in my Castle-hall:—" A maid, lovely as the Queen of Fairies, hung on my knee, and hailed me by that sweet name, "Father!"—Yes, I was happy!— Yet frown not on me therefore, Darkness!—I am thine again, my gloomy bride!—Be not incensed, Despair, that I left thee for a moment; I have passed with thee sixteen years! Ah! how many have I still to pass?—Yet fly not my bosom quite, sweet Hope!—Still speak to me of liberty, of light!—Whisper, that once more I shall see the morn break—that again shall my fevered lips drink the pure gale of evening!—(. . .) Let me once again press my daughter in my arms!—Let me, for one instant, feel again that I clasp to my heart a being that loves me!—Speed thou to heaven, prayer of a captive!—

The Cherry Orchard

Anton Chekhov

Translated by Mason W. Cartwright

Play
40s–50s
Dramatic

Gayev and his brother are resisting the sale of the cherry orchard for sentimental reasons, even though its sale would save the family from financial straits. Here, Gayev makes a passionate resolution he cannot keep.

I was at the district court on Thursday and I talked to some people about our problem and it looks as though we might be able to get a loan to pay the interest. I'm going back on Tuesday and talk to them again. And your mother's going to talk to Lopakhin. He won't turn her down. And after you've rested, you'll go see your great aunt, the countess, in Yaroslavl. This way we'll be attacking the problem from all sides—we can't miss. I'm sure we'll pay off the interest. I give you my word of honor, I'll swear on anything you want, this estate will not be sold! I swear on my own happiness! Here's my hand on it. You can call me a worthless scoundrel if I let this estate come up for auction. I'd die before I'd let it happen.

The Cherry Orchard

Anton Chekhov
Translated by Mason W. Cartwright

Play
40s-50s
Dramatic

Trofimov uses the cherry orchard as an analogy for Russia's shameful past, and he states that redemption will be found only in work.

All of Russia is our orchard. Our land is vast and beautiful, and full of wonderful places. Just think of it, Anya, your grandfather, your great-grandfather, all of your ancestors, owned slaves, actually owned human souls. Look! From every cherry tree in the orchard, from every leaf, from every trunk, generations of human beings are looking at you. Listen! You can hear their voices. Owning human souls has had its effect on all of you—your ancestors living and dead! You're in debt, all of you, your mother, your uncle, even you are in debt and are living at the expense of other people; people you won't even let in your house. We're two hundred years behind the times, we've made no progress, and we don't have the slightest idea of our relation to the past. All we are are bored complainers who sit around and philosophize and drink vodka! It's clear if we're going to live in the present that we've got to first redeem our past (. . .) by suffering and committing ourselves to work, to honest, endless work! Understand, Anya?

The Cherry Orchard

Anton Chekhov

Translated by Mason W. Cartwright

Play
50s
Dramatic

In a supremely ironic twist, Lopakhin reveals that he purchased the cherry orchard at auction, a disclosure that sends shock waves through the family.

Good Lord, the cherry orchard is mine! Tell me I'm drunk, tell me I'm dreaming! Don't laugh! If only my father and grandfather could rise up out of their graves and see me now: see their little Yermolai now, their ignorant little Yermolai who was always getting beaten, who ran barefoot all winter. If they could only see how I went out and just bought this estate, the most beautiful place in the world! An estate where my father and grandfather weren't even allowed in the kitchen, where they were slaves! It's all a dream, it must be! I'm asleep, I'm imagining! It can't be true!

Varya threw down the keys because she knows she's no longer in charge of the house. So, so what? Ah! The musicians. Go ahead musicians, play, I want to hear you! Come on everybody, come see Yermolai Lopakhin take an axe to the cherry orchard, come and see the trees come crashing down! We're going to build summer cottages, and our grandchildren and great-grandchildren are going to know a new life! Play musicians, play!

The Czar's Soliloquy
Mark Twain

Original Monologue
45+
Comic

"After the Czar's morning bath, it is his habit to meditate an hour before dressing himself."

—London Times Correspondence, 1905

(*Viewing himself in the pier-glass.*) Naked, what am I? A lank, skinny, spider-legged libel on the image of God! Look at the waxwork head—the face, with the expression of a melon—the projecting ears—the knotted elbows—the dished breast—the knife-edged shins—and then the feet, all beads and joints and bone-sprays, an imitation X-ray photograph! There is nothing imperial about this, nothing imposing, impressive, nothing to invoke awe and reverence. Is it this that a hundred and forty million Russians kiss the dust before and worship? Manifestly not! No one could worship this spectacle, which is Me. Then who is it, what is it, that they worship? Privately, none knows better than I: it is my clothes. Without my clothes I should be as destitute of authority as any other naked person. Nobody could tell me from a parson, a barber, a dude. Then who is the real Emperor of Russia? My clothes. There is no other.

Darnley
Edward Bulwer-Lytton

Play
30s
Dramatic

*When Darnley's spoiled wife tells him she wants a separation,
Darnley rues the day he married her.*

Oh! let man beware of marriage until he thoroughly know the
mind of her on whom his future must depend. Woe to him,
agony and woe, when the wife feels no sympathy with the toil,
when she soothes not in the struggle, when her heart is far from
that world within, to which her breath gives the life, and her
presence is the sun! How many men in humbler life have fled,
from a cheerless hearth to the haunts of guilt! How many in the
convict's exile, in the felon's cell, might have shunned the fall—
if woman (whom Heaven meant for our better angel) had
allured their step from the first paths to hell by making a paradise of home! (. . .) Look round the gay world you live in, and
when you see the faithless husband wasting health, fortune,
honor, in unseemly vices--behold too often the cause of all in
the cold eyes and barren heart of the fashionable wife.

Doctor Faustus
Christopher Marlowe

Play
35+
Dramatic

Faustus, at the end of his damned life.

Ah, Faustus.
Now hast thou but one bare hour to live,
And then thou must be damn'd perpetually!
Stand still, you ever-moving spheres of heaven,
That time may cease, and midnight never come;
Fair Nature's eye, rise, rise again, and make
Perpetual day; or let this hour be but
A year, a month, a week, a natural day,
That Faustus may repent and save his soul!
O lente, lente currite, noctis equi!
The stars move still, time runs, the clock will strike,
The devil will come, and Faustus must be damn'd.
O, I'll leap up to my God!—Who pulls me down?—
See, see, where Christ's blood streams in the firmament!
One drop would save my soul, half a drop: ah, my Christ!—
Ah, rend not my heart for naming of my Christ!
Yet will I call on him: O, spare me, Lucifer!—
Where is it now? tis gone: and see, where God
Stretcheth out his arm, and bends his ireful brows!
Mountains and hills, come, come, and fall on me,
And hide me from the heavy wrath of God!
No, no!

Don Quixote
Miguel de Cervantes

Novel
30s+
Dramatic

The faithful squire, Sancho Panza begs a dying Don Quixote to live.

Alas! good sir, [*replied Sancho*] do not die, I pray you; but take my advice, and live many years: for the greatest folly a man can commit in this world, is to give himself up to death, without any good cause for it, but only from melancholy. Good your worship, be not idle, but rise and let us be going to the field, dressed like shepherds, as we agreed to do: and who knows but behind some bush or other we may find the lady Dulcinea disenchanted as fine as heart can wish? If you pine at being vanquished, lay the blame upon me, and say you were unhorsed because I had not duly girthed Rozinante's saddle; and your worship must have seen in your books of chivalry that nothing is more common than for one knight to unhorse another, and that he who is vanquished today may be the conqueror to morrow.

The Green Cockatoo
Arthur Schnitzler
Translated by Grace Isabel Colbron

Play
25+
Dramatic

Henri confesses his crime of passion.

I accompanied her to the theater—it was to be the last time—I kissed her—at the door. She went up to her dressing room—I walked away like a man who has nothing to fear. But scarce a hundred paces from the house—it began in me—do you understand?—a horrible unease—something pulled and tugged at me to go back—and I did turn and go back. Then I was ashamed and walked away again—and again I was a hundred paces from the theater—and again it seized me and tore me—and I returned again. Her scene was over—she hasn't much to do— she stands a short time on the stage—half naked—and then she is through. I stood before her dressing room—I put my ear to the door and listened—I heard whispering—I could not hear the words. The whispering stopped—I broke open the door. It was the Duke de Cadignan—and I killed him—

The Hairy Ape
Eugene O'Neill

Play
30+
Dramatic

Yank, a coal stoker on a steamship, rejects Biblical damnation.

Sit down before I knock yuh down! *(LONG makes haste to efface himself. YANK goes on contemptuously.)* De Bible, huh? De Cap'tlist class, huh? Aw nix on dat Salvation Army–Socialist bull. Git a soapbox! Hire a hall! Come and be saved, huh? Jerk us to Jesus, huh? Aw g'wan! I've listened to lots of guys like you, see? You're all wrong. Wanter know what I t'ink? Yuh ain't no good for no one. Yuh're de bunk. Yuh ain't got no noive, get me? Yuh're yellow, dat's what. Yellow, dat's you. Say! What's dem slobs in de foist cabin got to do wit us? We're better men dan dey are, ain't we? Sure! One of us guys could clean up de whole mob wit one mit. Put one of 'em down here for one watch in de stokehole, what'd happen? Dey'd carry him off on a stretcher. Dem boids don't amount to nothin'. Dey're just baggage. Who makes dis old tub run? Ain't it us guys? Well den, we belong, don't we? We belong and dey don't. Dat's all. As for dis bein' hell—aw, nuts! Yuh lost your noive, dat's what. Dis is a man's job, get me? It belongs. It runs dis tub. No stiffs need apply. But yuh're a stiff, see? Yuh're yellow, dat's you.

Hamlet
William Shakespeare

Play
50s+
Dramatic

The ghost of Hamlet's father reveals he was murdered, and bids Hamlet to avenge him.

I am thy father's spirit,
Doomed for a certain term to walk the night,
And for the day confined to fast in fires,
Till the foul crimes done in my days of nature
Are burnt and purged away. But that I am forbid
To tell the secrets of my prison house,
I could a tale unfold whose lightest word
Would harrow up thy soul, freeze thy young blood,
Make thy two eyes like stars start from their spheres,
Thy knotted and combinèd locks to part,
And each particular hair to stand on end
Like quills upon the fretful porpentine.
But this eternal blazon must not be
To ears of flesh and blood. List, list, O, list!
If thou didst ever thy dear father love,
Revenge his foul and most unnatural murder.
'Tis given out that, sleeping in my orchard,
A serpent stung me. So the whole ear of Denmark
Is by a forgèd process of my death
Rankly abused. But know, thou noble youth,
The serpent that did sting thy father's life
Now wears his crown. Thy uncle,

Ay, that incestuous, that adulterous beast,
With witchcraft of his wit, with traiterous gifts—
O wicked wit and gifts, that have the power
So to seduce!—won to his shameful lust
The will of my most seeming-virtuous queen.

Henry IV
William Shakespeare

Play
40s+
Comic

Falstaff advises the young Henry on the company he keeps.

Harry, I do not only marvel where thou spendest thy time, but also how thou art accompanied. For though the camomile, the more it is trodden on, the faster it grows, yet youth, the more it is wasted, the sooner it wears. That thou art my son I have partly thy mother's word, partly my own opinion, but chiefly a villainous trick of thine eye and a foolish hanging of thy nether lip that doth warrant me. If then thou be son to me, here lies the point: why, being son to me, art thou so pointed at? Shall the blessed sun of heaven prove a micher and eat blackberries? A question not to be asked. There is a thing, Harry, which thou hast often heard of, and it is known to many in our land by the name of pitch. This pitch, as ancient writers do report, doth defile; so doth the company thou keepest. For, Harry, now I do not speak to thee in drink, but in tears; not in pleasure, but in passion; not in words only, but in woes also: and yet there is a virtuous man whom I have often noted in thy company, but I know not his name. A goodly portly man, i' faith, and a corpulent; of a cheerful look, a pleasing eye, and a most noble carriage; and, as I think, his age some fifty, or, by'r Lady, inclining to threescore; and now I remember me, his name is Falstaff. If that man should be lewdly given he deceiveth me; for, Harry, I see virtue in his looks. If then the tree may be known by the fruit, as the fruit by the tree, then, peremptorily I speak it, there is virtue in that Falstaff. Him keep with, the rest banish.

Hindle Wakes

Stanley Houghton

Play
30s
Dramatic

Alan Jeffcote, a mill-owner's son, tries to explain to his would-be girlfriend, Beatrice, why he spent a scandalous weekend away with Fanny Hawthorn.

Of course I knew her before Blackpool. There's not so many pretty girls in Hindle that you can miss one like Fanny Hawthorn. I knew her well enough, but on the straight, mind you. I'd hardly spoken to her before I ran into her at the Tower in Blackpool. We'd just had dinner at the Metropole Grill-room, George and I, and I daresay had drunk about as much champagne as was good for us. We looked in at the Tower for a lark, and we ran into Fanny in the Ballroom. (. . .) What else do you want me to tell you?

Yes, Bee, I suppose I did think about you. But you weren't there, you see, and she was. That was what did it. Being near her and looking at her lips. Then I forgot everything else. Oh, I know. I'm a beast. I couldn't help it. I suppose you can never understand. It's too much for you to see the difference. Fanny was just an amusement—a lark. I thought of her as a girl to have a bit of fun with. Going off with her was like going off and getting tight for once in a way. You wouldn't care for me to do that, but if I did you wouldn't think very seriously about it. You wouldn't want to break off our engagement for that. I wonder if you can look on this affair of Fanny's as something like getting tight—only worse. I'm ashamed of myself, just as I should be if you caught me drunk. I can't defend myself.

Keep Your Own Secret
Pedro Calderón de la Barca

Play
20+
Dramatic

The Prince begs Don Arias to find out what ails his dear friend, Don Cesar.

Don Arias,
I love Don Cesar with as whole a heart
As ever. He and I from infancy
Have grown together; as one single soul
Our joys and sorrows shared; till finding him
So wise and true, as to another self
Myself, and my dominion to boot,
I did intrust: you are his friend, and surely
In honouring you I honour him as well.
Besides, Arias, I know not how it is,
For some while past a change has come on him;
I know not what the cause: he is grown sad,
Neglects his business—if I call to him,
He hears me not, or answers from the purpose,
Or in mid answer stops. And, by the way,
We being on this subject, I would fain,
Being so much his friend, for both our sakes,
You would find out what ails and occupies him;
Tell him from me to use my power as ever,
Absolute still: that, loving him so well,
I'd know what makes him so unlike himself;
That, knowing what it is, I may at least,
If not relieve his sorrow, share with him.

King John
William Shakespeare

Play
Teen
Dramatic

Arthur, the young imprisoned nephew of wicked King John, pleads with his keeper not to follow his uncle's orders—to put out his eyes.

Must you with hot irons burn out both mine eyes?
And will you?
Have you the heart? When your head did but ache
I knit my handkerchief about your brows,
The best I had, a princess wrought it me,
And I did never ask it you again;
And with my hand at midnight held your head,
And like the watchful minutes to the hour,
Still and anon cheer'd up the heavy time,
Saying 'What lack you?' and 'Where lies your grief?'
Or 'What good love may I perform for you?'
Many a poor man's son would have lain still
And ne'er have spoke a loving word to you;
But you, at your sick service, had a prince.
Nay, you may think my love was crafty love
And call it cunning: do, an if you will,
If heaven be pleas'd that you must use me ill,
Why then you must. Will you put out mine eyes?
These eyes that never did nor never shall
So much as frown on you?

Lady Windermere's Fan
Oscar Wilde

Play
20s
Dramatic

Lord Darling, professional cad, lays it on thick to Lady Windermere.

Yes, I love you! You are more to me than anything in the whole world. What does your husband give you? Nothing. Whatever is in him he gives to this wretched woman, whom he has thrust into your society, into your home, to shame you before everyone. I offer you my life—(. . .) I love you—love you as I have never loved any living thing. From the moment I met you I loved you, loved you blindly, adoringly, madly! You did not know it then—you know it now! Leave this house to-night. I won't tell you that the world matters nothing, or the world's voice, or the voice of society. They matter a good deal. They matter far too much. But there are moments when one has to choose between living one's own life, fully, entirely, completely— or dragging out some false, shallow, degrading existence that the world in its hypocrisy demands. You have that moment now. Choose! Oh, my love, choose!

Living Hours

Arthur Schnitzler
Translated by Grace Isabel Colbron

Play
30+
Dramatic

Rademacher, with nothing to lose, reveals all to his acquaintance.

You think yourself better than I? My dear friend, you and I are not great men, and in the depths where we belong there is little difference—in hours like these. All your greatness is sham and pretense. Your fame? Merely a heap of newspaper notices that will be scattered to the winds the day after your death. Your friends? Flatterers who flock to success; envious parasites who clench their fists at you when your back is turned; fools who find you just small enough for their admiration. But you are clever enough to realize all this yourself, at times. I didn't trouble to come here just to tell you that. What I am going to tell you—it may be despicable of me—but it's astonishing how little we care whether we are despicable or not when we know we'll have no tomorrow to be ashamed of it in . . . I've come near throwing it in your face a hundred times during the past few years—whenever we chanced to meet on the street and you were gracious enough to stop for a few words with me. My dear friend, not only do I know you as you are—and hundreds of others do, too—but your own beloved wife knows you better than you dream. She realized what you were twenty years ago—in the prime of your youth and success. Yes, she realized it—and I knew that she did—for I was her lover two whole years.

The Lower Depths
Maxim Gorky
Translated by Laurence Irving

Play
40+
Dramatic

Now residing in a flophouse of degenerates, a former Baron questions the meaning of his life.

You know . . . from when first I can remember . . . there's been inside my noodle a sort of fog. Never anything have I understood. I'm . . . in some way—I'm clumsy. It seems to me all my life I've done nothing but dress up . . . and why? Went to school—wore the uniform of the Institute for the Sons of the Nobility . . . but what did I learn? Don't remember. . . . Married—in a frock-coat, and an over-coat . . . but I picked the wrong wife and—why? Don't understand . . . Squandered all I had, wore some sort of a grey pea-jacket and red trousers . . . but where did it all get to? Never noticed . . . Entered the Court of Exchequer . . . uniform, and a cap with a cockade . . . made away with some Government money—they put me into the convict's gown . . . then—I got into this lot here . . . And all . . . like in a dream . . . ah? That's funny . . . *(Pause.)* But I must have been born for some reason . . . Eh?

The Merchant of Venice
William Shakespeare

Play
40+
Dramatic

Shylock makes his case for revenge, a lesson learned from his own experience.

He hath disgraced me, and hindered me half a million; laughed at my losses, mocked at my gains, scorned my nation, thwarted my bargains, cooled my friends, heated mine enemies; and what's his reason? I am a Jew.

Hath not a Jew eyes? Hath not a Jew hands, organs, dimensions, senses, affections, passions? Fed with the same food, hurt with the same weapons, subject to the same diseases, healed by the same means, warmed and cooled by the same winter and summer, as a Christian is?

If you prick us, do we not bleed? If you tickle us, do we not laugh? If you poison us, do we not die? And if you wrong us, shall we not revenge? If we are like you in the rest, we will resemble you in that.

If a Jew wrong a Christian, what is his humility . . . ? Revenge.

If a Christian wrong a Jew, what should his sufferance be by Christian example? Why, revenge.

The villany you teach me, I will execute, and it shall go hard . . . but I will better the instruction.

A Midsummer Night's Dream

William Shakespeare

Play
35+
Dramatic

Theseus weighs the consequences should Hermia obey or dis-
obey her father's order to marry Demetrius.

Either to die the death, or to abjure
For ever the society of men.
Therefore, fair Hermia, question your desires,
Know of your youth, examine well your blood,
Whether, if you yield not to your father's choice,
You can endure the livery of a nun.
Take time to pause; and by the next new moon,
The sealing-day betwixt my love and me
For everlasting bond of fellowship,
Upon that day either prepare to die
For disobedience to your father's will,
Or else to wed Demetrius, as he would,
Or on Diana's altar to protest,
For aye, austerity and single life.

A Midsummer Night's Dream

William Shakespeare

Play
30s+
Comic

Oberon, King of the Fairies, enlists Puck in playing a trick on his Queen, Titania.

My gentle Puck, come hither. Thou rememb'rest
Since once I sat upon a promontory,
And heard a mermaid on a dolphin's back
Uttering such dulcet and harmonious breath
That the rude sea grew civil at her song?
That very time I saw (but thou couldst not),
Flying between the cold moon and the earth,
Cupid all arm'd: a certain aim he took
Yet mark'd I where the bolt of Cupid fell:
It fell upon a little western flower,
Before milk-white, now purple with love's wound:
And maidens call it 'love-in-idleness'.
Fetch me that flower; the herb I show'd thee once.
The juice of it, on sleeping eyelids laid,
Will make or man or woman madly dote
Upon the next live creature that it sees.

A Midsummer Night's Dream

William Shakespeare

Play
20s+
Comic

Bottom, whom Puck turned into a donkey, wakes up restored and thinks he dozed off during a rehearsal.

When my cue comes, call me and I will answer. My next is "Most fair Pyramus." Heigh-ho! Peter Quince? Flute, the bellows-mender? Snout, the tinker? Starveling? God's my life! Stolen hence, and left me asleep! *(To himself.)* I have had a most rare vision. I have had a dream, past the wit of man to say what dream it was. Man is but an ass if he go about to expound this dream. Methought I was—and methought I had—the eye of man hath not heard, the ear of man hath not seen, what my dream was. I will get Peter Quince to write a ballad of this dream: it shall be called "Bottom's Dream", because it hath no bottom; and I will sing it in the latter end of a play, before the Duke.

A Midsummer Night's Dream
William Shakespeare

Play
20+
Comic

Puck taunts us with the possibility that the story we've just watched was but a dream.

If we shadows have offended,
Think but this, and all is mended,
That you have but slumber'd here
While these visions did appear.
And this weak and idle theme,
No more yielding but a dream,
Gentles, do not reprehend:
if you pardon, we will mend:
And, as I am an honest Puck,
If we have unearned luck
Now to 'scape the serpent's tongue,
We will make amends ere long;
Else the Puck a liar call;
So, good night unto you all.
Give me your hands, if we be friends,
And Robin shall restore amends.

A Midsummer Night's Dream

William Shakespeare

Play
35+
Comic

Duke Theseus makes the comparison between those in love and the mentally disturbed.

Lovers and madmen have such seething brains,
Such shaping fantasies, that apprehend
More than cool reason ever comprehends.
The lunatic, the lover, and the poet
Are of imagination all compact.
One sees more devils than vast hell can hold;
That is the madman.   The lover, all as frantic,
Sees Helen's beauty in a brow of Egypt.
The poet's eye, in a fine frenzy rolling,
Doth glance from heaven to earth, from earth to heaven.
And as imagination bodies forth
The forms of things unknown, the poet's pen
Turns them to shapes, and gives to airy nothing
A local habitation, and a name.
Such tricks hath strong imagination,
That if it would but apprehend some joy,
It comprehends some bringer of that joy.
Or in the night, imagining some fear,
How easy is a bush supposed a bear.

The Misanthrope

Molière
Translated by Hal Gelb

Play
25+
Comic

*Alceste speaks to Celimene, who asks if she should "beat her
admirers off with a stick."*

No, madam, there is no need for a stick, but only a heart less
yielding and less melting at their love-tales. I am aware that
your good looks accompany you, go where you will; but your
reception retains those whom your eyes attract; and that gentle-
ness, accorded to those who surrender their arms, finishes on
their hearts the sway which your charms began. The too agree-
able expectation which you offer them increases their assiduities
towards you; and your complacency, a little less extended,
would drive away the great crowd of so many admirers. But,
tell me, at least, madam, by what good fortune Clitandre has
the happiness of pleasing you so mightily? Upon what basis of
merit and sublime virtue do you ground the honour of your
regard for him?

The Misanthrope

Molière
Translated by Hal Gelb

Play
40s-50s
Comic

Acaste is one of the courtiers impoverished in Louis XIV's plan to break the aristocracy and put the middle class in positions of power. To replenish his bank account, he is trying to marry Celimene, the widow of a wealthy merchant. Here, he defends himself from an attack by Clitandre, a rival courtier. Nothing he says about himself is true.

Well, when I look at myself,
I don't see anything to be troubled about.
I'm young, healthy and sitting on oodles and oodles of wealth.
As to valor, by which men prove their honor
And everlasting worth, I've got it.
I think I can say that without being unduly immodest.
At the battle of St. Gotthard, I took the Turk's right flank
And Louis' undying thanks.
And I don't think I need to mention
I've got lots and lots of francs.
Then too, my mind is subtle, my figure sleek;
I have good bearing, good looks and unusually pretty teeth.
And as for the statement made by the way I dress,
Well, in its own quiet way, it invites patronage and success.
Yes, I'm loved by the king and deemed a total national treasure
By scores of women to whom I bring enormous pleasure.
And did I mention I have money beyond measure?

The Misanthrope

Molière
Translated by Hal Gelb

Play
Late 20s-30s
Comic

*Alceste, the "misanthrope," is madly in love with Celimene.
When Arsinoe shows him a letter, which she claims was written
by Celimene to a secret lover, Alceste's jealousy competes with
his love.*

My God! Has a loving heart ever been treated this way?
I'm the one with reason to complain,
It's her behavior that's been in offensive,
And in the end, I'm the one who finds himself on the defensive!
She makes me drink my pain in to the very last drop,
Encouraging my worst suspicions and glorying in it all nonstop.
And still my heart lacks resolve to break away
Or at least arm itself with a generous contempt
For this ingrate who infatuates me.
Perfidious woman, you really know how to use my weakness
    against me
And turn the fatal excess of my love to your advantage.
At least defend yourself.
Don't pretend you're guilty of a crime
That's choking the last little bit of life out of me.
If there's any way, show me that this letter's innocent.
If you'll only make an effort to seem faithful,
I'll do everything I can believing it.

Mithridate

Jean Racine
Translated by Robert Bruce Boswell

Play
30+
Dramatic

Mithridate scolds his spoiled princess for bringing up a past injustice.

Have you forgotten, false, ungrateful woman,
Worse than the Romans, my sworn enemies,
From what exalted rank I dared to stoop,
To offer you a throne, little expected?
See me not as I am, defeated, hunted—
But as I was, victorious and renown'd.
Think how in Ephesus I you preferr'd
To all the daughters of a hundred kings,
And, for your sake neglecting their alliance,
Laid at your feet innumerable realms. (. . .)
And now, when I am willing to forgive
The grievous wrong and bury its remembrance,
Dare you to bring the past before my eyes
Again, accusing him whom you have injured?
I see infatuation for a traitor
Flatters your hopes. Gods! How ye try my patience!

The Octoroon
Dion Boucicault

Play
30s
Dramatic

The evil slave owner, McClusky, is hiding in the swamp, pursued for murder. Here, he wakes from a nightmare, paranoid, desperate, and jumpy.

Burn, burn! blaze away! How the flames crack. I'm not guilty; would ye murder me? Cut, cut the rope—I choke -choke! Ah! *(Wakes.)* Hello! where am I? Why, I was dreaming —curse it! I can never sleep now without dreaming. Hush! I thought I heard the sound of a paddle in the water. All night as I fled through the canebrake, I heard footsteps behind me. I lost them in the cedar swamp—resting when I rested—hush! There again!—no; it was only the wind over the canes. The sun is rising. (. . .) In a little time this darned business will blow over, and I can show again. Hark! there's that noise again! It it was the ghost of that murdered boy haunting me! Well—I didn't mean to kill him, did I? Well, then, what has my all-cowardly heart got to skeer me so for?

The Open Boat
Stephen Crane

Short Story
25+
Dramatic

Three men survive a shipwreck and struggle to get to shore in an open boat.

[As for the reflections of the men, there was a great deal of rage in them. Perchance they might be formulated thus:]

If I am going to be drowned—if I am going to be drowned—if I am going to be drowned, why, in the name of the seven mad gods who rule the sea, was I allowed to come thus far and contemplate sand and trees? Was I brought here merely to have my nose dragged away as I was about to nibble the sacred cheese of life? It is preposterous. If this old ninny woman, Fate, cannot do better than this, she should be deprived of the management of men's fortunes. She is an old hen who knows not her intention. If she has decided to drown me, why did she not do it in the beginning and save me all this trouble? The whole affair is absurd . . . But no, she cannot mean to drown me. She dare not drown me. She cannot drown me. Not after all this work.

[Afterward the man might have had an impulse to shake his fist at the clouds:]

Just you drown me, now, and then hear what I call you!

Othello

William Shakespeare

Play
35+
Dramatic

Iago, convinced Desdemona has committed adultery, snaps when she asks ". . . what ignorant sin have I committed?"

Was this fair paper, this most goodly book,
Made to write 'whore' upon? What committed!
Committed! O thou public commoner!
I should make very forges of my cheeks,
That would to cinders burn up modesty,
Did I but speak thy deeds. What committed!
Heaven stops the nose at it and the moon winks,
The bawdy wind that kisses all it meets
Is hush'd within the hollow mine of earth,
And will not hear it. What committed!
Impudent strumpet!

Othello
William Shakespeare

Play
30s
Dramatic

Iago plots to make Othello jealous.

That Cassio loves her, I do well believe it;
That she loves him, 'tis apt and of great credit:
The Moor, howbeit that I endure him not,
Is of a constant, loving, noble nature,
And I dare think he'll prove to Desdemona
A most dear husband. Now, I do love her too;
Not out of absolute lust, though peradventure
I stand accountant for as great a sin,
But partly led to diet my revenge,
For that I do suspect the lusty Moor
Hath leap'd into my seat; the thought whereof
Doth, like a poisonous mineral, gnaw my inwards;
And nothing can or shall content my soul
Till I am even'd with him, wife for wife,
Or failing so, yet that I put the Moor
At least into a jealousy so strong
That judgment cannot cure. Which thing to do,
If this poor trash of Venice, whom I trash
For his quick hunting, stand the putting on,
I'll have our Michael Cassio on the hip,
Abuse him to the Moor in the rank garb—
For I fear Cassio with my night-cap too—
Make the Moor thank me, love me and reward me.

For making him egregiously an ass
And practising upon his peace and quiet
Even to madness. 'Tis here, but yet confused:
Knavery's plain face is never seen till used.

Philoctetes
Sophocles

Play
30+
Dramatic

Neoptolemus, son of Achilles' has taken Heracles away from Philoctetes. Here, Philoctetes bemoans the loss.

O thou fire!
Thou universal horror! Masterpiece
Abominable, of monstrous villainy!
What hast thou done to me? How hast thou cheated me!
Art not ashamed, O rogue, to look at me
Thy supplicant, me thy petitioner?
Thou has robbed me of my life, taking my bow.
Give it back, I beg thee! Give it back, I pray!
By our father's gods, son, do not take my life!
Woe's me! he does not even answer me!
He means to keep it—see, he turns away! (. . .)
See how Achilles' son is wronging me! (. . .)
What say'st thou? Thou art dumb! I am lost, unhappy! (. . .)
Creatures I chased before will now chase me;
And I shall pay for bloodshed with my blood,
By practice of a seeming innocent!
O may'st thou perish!—not yet, until I know
Whether thou wilt repent, and change thy purpose;
But if thou wilt not, evil be thine end!

The Prince of Parthia

Thomas Godfrey

Play
20s
Dramatic

Vardanes, jealous of his older brother, believes himself more deserving of his father's empire.

I hate *Arsaces*,
Tho' he's my Mother's son, and churchmen say
There's something sacred in the name of Brother.
My soul endures him not, and he's the bane
Of all my hopes of greatness. Like the sun
He rules the day, and like the night's pale Queen,
My fainter beams are lost when he appears.
And this because he came into the world,
A moon or two before me: What's the diff'rence,
That he alone should shine in Empire's seat?
I am not apt to trumpet forth my praise.
Or highly name myself, but this I'll speak,
To him in ought, I'm not the least inferior.
Ambition, glorious fever! mark of Kings,
Gave me immortal thirst and rule of Empire.
Why lag'd my tardy soul, why droop'd the wing,
Nor forward springing, shot before his speed
To seize the prize?—'Twas Empire—
Oh! 'twas Empire—

The Provoked Wife
Sir John Vanbrugh

Play
20s
Seriocomic

After two years of marriage, Sir John is ready to do something drastic.

What cloying meat is love, when matrimony's the sauce to it. Two years' marriage has debauched my five senses. Everything I see, taste, everything I hear, everything I feel, everything I smell, and everything I taste, methinks has wife in't. No body was ever so weary of his tutor, no girl of her bib, no nun of doing penance, nor old maid of being chaste, as I am of being married. Sure there's a secret curse entailed upon the very name of wife. My lady is a young lady, a fine lady, a witty lady, a virtuous lady, and yet I hate her. There is but one thing on earth I loathe beyond her: that's fighting. Would my courage come up but to a fourth part of my ill nature, I'd stand buff to her relations, and thrust her out of doors. But marriage has sunk me down to such an ebb of resolution, I dare not draw my sword, though even to get rid of my wife. But here she comes.

Reigen

Arthur Schnitzler
Translated by Grace Isabel Colbron

Play
30+
Comic

After a bender, the Count wakes up in a woman's bed.

(Stirs, rubs his eyes, sits up quickly, looks about him.) Where am I? . . . Oh yes . . . So I did go home with the woman after all . . . *(Gets up, sees her in bed.)* There she lies . . God, the things that can happen to a man of my age. I haven't the faintest idea, did they carry me up here, I wonder? No . . . I remember seeing—I came into the room . . . yes . . . I was still awake then, or had just waked up . . . or . . . is it just that this room reminds me of something? . . . 'pon my soul, yes . . . I did see it all yesterday . . . *(Looks at his watch.)* Yesterday hell! . . . a few hours ago— But I knew something was bound to happen . . . I felt it coming . . . .When I began drinking yesterday I felt that . . . but what did happen, anyway? . . . Nothing, maybe . . . Or did it . . . ? 'Pon my soul . . . since . . . well, for ten years this sort of thing hasn't happened to me, not knowing what . . . Oh well, the whole point is that I was good and drunk . . . (. . .) The main thing is to get out. *(Stands up. The lamp shakes.)* Oh! *(Looks at the sleeping woman.)* She sleeps soundly enough. I don't remember a damn thing—but I'll leave some money on the night-table . . . and beat it. (. . .) Hm, I'd just like to know whether . . . no, I would have remembered that . . . no, no, I collapsed on the sofa right away . . . and nothing happened . . . It's incredible how all women look alike sometimes . . . well, let's move along.

Richard III
William Shakespeare

Play
30s+
Dramatic

Richard gloats over his use of power, lies, and crime to obtain the woman he desires, Queen Anne.

Was ever woman in this humour woo'd?
Was ever woman in this humour won?
I'll have her; but I will not keep her long.
What! I, that kill'd her husband and his father,
To take her in her heart's extremest hate,
With curses in her mouth, tears in her eyes,
The bleeding witness of her hatred by;
Having God, her conscience, and these bars
against me,
And I nothing to back my suit at all,
But the plain devil and dissembling looks,
And yet to win her, all the world to nothing!
Ha! (. . .)
My dukedom to a beggarly denier,
I do mistake my person all this while:
Upon my life, she finds, although I cannot,
Myself to be a marvellous proper man.
I'll be at charges for a looking-glass,
And entertain some score or two of tailors,
To study fashions to adorn my body:
Since I am crept in favour with myself,
Will maintain it with some little cost.

But first I'll turn yon fellow in his grave;
And then return lamenting to my love.
Shine out, fair sun, till I have bought a glass,
That I may see my shadow as I pass.

The Rivals
Richard Brinsley Sheridan

Play
Late 20s-30s
Comic

Having wrongly accused Julia of infidelity (causing her to storm out in tears), Faukland's two sides wrestle: maintain his macho indignation or be a romantic puppy dog?

In tears! Stay, Julia: stay but for a moment.—The door is fastened!—Julia;—my soul—but for one moment:—I hear her sobbing!—'Sdeath! What a brute am I to use her thus! Yet stay!—Aye—she is coming now:—how little resolution there is in woman!—How a few soft words can turn them!—No, faith!—she is *not* coming either.—Why, Julia—my love—say but that you forgive me—come but to tell me that. —Now, this is being *too* resentful:—stay! She *is* coming too—I thought she would—no *steadiness* in anything! Her going away must have been a mere trick then.—She sha'n't see that I was hurt by it.—I'll affect indifference.—(*Hums a tune: then listens.*)— No—Zounds! She's *not* coming!—nor don't intend it, I suppose.—This is not *steadiness*, but *obstinacy*! Yet I deserve it.—what, after so long an absence, to quarrel with her tenderness!—'twas barbarous and unmanly!—I should be ashamed to see her now.—I'll wait till her just resentment is abated—and when I distress her so again, may I lose her for ever! And be linked instead to some antique virago, whose gnawing passions, and long-hoarded spleen, shall make me curse my folly half the day, and all the night!

Romeo and Juliet
William Shakespeare

Play
20s
Seriocomic

*Romeo's friend, Mercutio, teases him about the romantic
dreams he's had.*

O, then, I see Queen Mab hath been with you.
She is the fairies' midwife, and she comes
In shape no bigger than an agate-stone
On the fore-finger of an alderman,
Drawn with a team of little atomies
Athwart men's noses as they lie asleep;
Her wagon-spokes made of long spiders' legs,
The cover of the wings of grasshoppers,
The traces of the smallest spider's web,
The collars of the moonshine's watery beams,
Her whip of cricket's bone, the lash of film,
Her wagoner a small grey-coated gnat,
Not so big as a round little worm
Prick'd from the lazy finger of a maid;
Her chariot is an empty hazel-nut
Made by the joiner squirrel or old grub,
Time out o' mind the fairies' coachmakers.
And in this state she gallops night by night
Through lovers' brains, and then they dream of love (. . .)

A Room with a View
E. M. Forster

Novel
60s+
Comic

The endearing Mr. Emerson finally confronts Miss Honeychurch with the fact that she does, indeed, love his son George.

My dear, I am worried about you. It seems to me—(. . .) that you are in a muddle. (. . .)

Take an old man's word; there's nothing worse than a muddle in all the world. It is easy to face Death and Fate, and the things that sound so dreadful. It is on my muddles that I look back with horror—on the things that I might have avoided. We can help one another but little. I used to think I could teach young people the whole of life, but I know better now, and all my teaching of George has come down to this: beware of muddle. Do you remember in that church when you pretended to be annoyed with me and weren't? Do you remember before, when you refused the room with the view? Those were muddles—little, but ominous—and I am fearing that you are in one now. (. . .)

"Life," wrote a friend of mine, "is a public performance on the violin, in which you must learn the instrument as you go along." I think he puts it well. Man has to pick up the use of his functions as he goes along—especially the function of Love. (. . .) That's it; that's what I mean. You love George! (. . .) You love the boy body and soul, plainly, directly, as he loves you, and no other word expresses it.

The School for Wives

Molière

Translated by Henri van Laun

Play
30+
Comic

Arnolphe, who thinks highly of himself, schools his wife-to-be on wifely ways.

Agnes, put your work down, and listen to me. Raise your head a little, and turn your face round. *(Putting his finger on his forehead.)* There, look at me here while I speak, and take good note of even the smallest word. I am going to wed you, Agnes; you ought to bless your stars a hundred times a day, to think of your former low estate, and at the same time, to wonder at my goodness in raising you from a poor country girl to the honourable rank of a citizen's wife; to enjoy the bed and the embraces of a man who has shunned all such trammels, and whose heart has refused to a score of women, well fitted to please, the honour which he intends to confer on you. You must always keep in mind, I say, how insignificant you would be without this glorious alliance, in order that the picture may teach you the better to merit the condition in which I shall place you, and make you always know yourself, so that I may never repent of what I am doing. Marriage, Agnes, is no joke. (. . .) I am not telling you a parcel of stories; you ought to let these lessons sink into your heart. (. . .) Make a curtsey.

The Sea Gull

Anton Chekhov

Translation by Mason W. Cartwright

Play
25
Seriocomic

Treplev, a young playwright and director, has trouble negotiating his drama-queen of a mother.

Mother is bored. And jealous. She's against me and the play and performance because Nina's in it and she isn't. She already hates the play and doesn't know a thing about it. And she's mad because, even on this tiny stage, Nina will be a hit and she won't. My mother—the mental case. Oh, she's talented all right, no doubt about it—and intelligent. She can cry her eyes out over a book, reel off all of Nekrasov's poems from memory, and if someone's sick, she'll take care of him like an angel . . . But just try to praise Duse in front of her! Oh boy! Watch out! You can only praise Mother, and write glowing reviews about her and rave about her performances in *The Lady with the Camellias* or *It's a Mad Life.* Out here in the country, where she's not getting praise all the time, she's bored and cross and everybody is her enemy. And she's superstitious, too; afraid of three candles burning and the number thirteen and things like that. And she's stingy. I know for a fact she has seventy thousand rubles in a bank in Odessa. But ask her for a loan and see what happens. She'll break down and cry like a baby.

The Sea Gull

Anton Chekhov

Translation by Mason W. Cartwright

Play
25
Seriocomic

Treplev, a young playwright and director, sifts through his troubles in the company of his uncle, Sorin.

(*Plucking petals from a flower.*) She loves me, she loves me not, she loves me, she loves me not, she loves me, she loves me not. (*Laughs.*) You see—Mother doesn't love me. Why should she? All I am is a twenty-five-year-old reminder that she's no longer a young woman. When I'm not around, she's only thirty-two, when I am, she's forty-three, and she hates me for it. And to make it worse, she knows I don't accept the theater. She loves the theater and thinks she's serving mankind and the sacred cause of art. As far as I'm concerned, the theater's stuck in the past. It's the same old stuff. The audience is looking through a fourth wall at an artificially lit set at artists who are the guardians of a sacred art, depicting how people eat and drink and work some little, cozy, easy-to-grasp moral suitable for home consumption. When they hand me the same old rehash time after boring time, that's when I run. Like Maupassant did when he saw the Eiffel Tower because he knew it would corrupt his mind.

Sonnet XVIII
William Shakespeare

Poem
20+
Dramatic

*The speaker searches for the perfect analogy to describe his
love's eternal beauty.*

Shall I compare thee to a summer's day?
Thou art more lovely and more temperate:
Rough winds do shake the darling buds of May,
And summer's lease hath all too short a date:
Sometime too hot the eye of heaven shines,
And often is his gold complexion dimmed,
And every fair from fair sometime declines,
By chance, or nature's changing course untrimmed:
But thy eternal summer shall not fade,
Nor lose possession of that fair thou ow'st,
Nor shall death brag thou wander'st in his shade,
When in eternal lines to time thou grow'st,
So long as men can breathe, or eyes can see,
So long lives this, and this gives life to thee.

Sonnet XXVIII

William Shakespeare

Poem
60+
Dramatic

*The speaker acknowledges his advancing age, and how it may
intensify his lover's affections.*

That time of year thou mayst in me behold
When yellow leaves, or none, or few, do hang
Upon those boughs which shake against the cold,
Bare ruined choirs, where late the sweet birds sang.
In me thou see'st the twilight of such day
As after sunset fadeth in the west;
Which by and by black night doth take away,
Death's second self, that seals up all in rest.
In me thou see'st the glowing of such fire,
That on the ashes of his youth doth lie,
As the deathbed whereon it must expire,
Consumed with that which it was nourished by.
This thou perceiv'st, which makes thy love more strong,
To love that well which thou must leave ere long.

Sonnet XXX
William Shakespeare

Poem
40s+
Dramatic

The speaker looks back on life and its sorrows.

When to the sessions of sweet, silent thought
I summon up remembrances of things past,
I sigh the lack of many a thing I sought,
And with old woes new wail my dear time's waste;
Then can I drown an eye (unused to flow)
For precious friends hid in death's dateless night,
And weep afresh love's long since cancelled woe,
And moan the expense of many a vanished sight.
Thus can I grieve at grievances foregone,
And heavily from woe to woe tell o'er
The sad account of fore bemoaned moan,
Which I new pay, as if not paid before;
    But if the while I think on thee, dear friend,
    All losses are restored, and sorrows end.

Sudden Light
Dante Gabriel Rossetti

Poem
25+
Dramatic

Romantic déjà vu, and the endurance of love.

I have been here before,
But when or how I cannot tell:
I know the grass beyond the door,
The sweet keen smell,
The sighing sound, the lights around the shore.
You have been mine before,—
How long ago I may not know:
But just when at that swallow's soar
Your neck turn'd so,
Some veil did fall,—I knew it all of yore.
Has this been thus before?
And shall not thus time's eddying flight
Still with our lives our love restore
In death's despite,
And day and night yield one delight once more?

The Tempest
William Shakespeare

Play
50+
Dramatic

Prospero draws Act IV of this "dream play" to a close.

Our revels now are ended. These our actors,
As I fortold you, were all spirits, and
Are melted into air, into thin air,
And like the baseless fabric of this vision,
The cloud-capped towers, the gorgeous palaces,
The solemn temples, the great globe itself,
Yea, all which it inherit, shall dissolve,
And like this insubstantial pageant faded
Leave not a rack behind. We are such stuff
As dreams are made on; and our little life
Is rounded with a sleep.

Thirst
Eugene O'Neill

Play
30+
Dramatic

Having survived a ship's sinking, a man struggles to remember events.

It was in the salon. You were singing. You were very beautiful. I remember a woman on my right saying: "How pretty she is! I wonder if she is married?" Strange how some idiotic remark like that will stick in one's brain when all else is vague and confused. I was looking at you and wondering what kind of woman you were. You know I had never met you personally— only seen you in my walks around the deck. Then came the crash—that horrible dull crash. We were all thrown forward on the floor of the salon; then screams, oaths, fainting women, the hollow boom of a bulkhead giving way. (. . .) Somehow I got into a boat—but it was overloaded and was swamped immediately. I swam to another boat. They beat me off with the oars. (. . .) I became frenzied with terror. I swam. (. . .) I saw something white on the water before me. I clutched it—climbed on it. It was this raft. You and he were on it. I fainted. The whole thing is a horrible nightmare in my brain—but I remember clearly that idiotic remark of the woman in the salon.

Titus Andronicus
William Shakespeare

Play
50+
Dramatic

Titus has lost one hand, his daughter Lavinia has lost both. Seeking revenge for this and a host of other atrocities, he prepares to kill Tamara's sons.

O villains, Chiron and Demetrius!
Here stands the spring whom you have stain'd with mud,
This goodly summer with your winter mix'd.
You kill'd her husband, and for that vile fault
Two of her brothers were condemn'd to death,
My hand cut off and made a merry jest;
Both her sweet hands, her tongue, and that more dear
Than hands or tongue, her spotless chastity,
Inhuman traitors, you constrain'd and forced.
What would you say, if I should let you speak?
Villains, for shame you could not beg for grace.
Hark, wretches! how I mean to martyr you.
This one hand yet is left to cut your throats,
Whilst that Lavinia 'tween her stumps doth hold
The basin that receives your guilty blood.
You know your mother means to feast with me,
And calls herself Revenge, and thinks me mad:
Hark, villains! I will grind your bones to dust
And with your blood and it I'll make a paste,
And of the paste a coffin I will rear
And make two pasties of your shameful heads,

And bid that strumpet, your unhallow'd dam,
Like to the earth swallow her own increase.
This is the feast that I have bid her to,
And this the banquet she shall surfeit on.

The Two Gentlemen of Verona

William Shakespeare

Play
20s
Comic

Proteus schemes to betray his friend, Valentine, in order to steal his girlfriend.

To leave my Julia, shall I be forsworn;
To love fair Silvia, shall I be forsworn;
To wrong my friend, I shall be much forsworn;
And even that power which gave me first my oath
Provokes me to this threefold perjury;
Love bade me swear and Love bids me forswear.
O sweet-suggesting Love, if thou hast sinned,
Teach me, thy tempted subject, to excuse it!
At first I did adore a twinkling star,
But now I worship a celestial sun.
I will forget that Julia is alive,
Remembering that my love to her is dead;
And Valentine I'll hold an enemy.

CONTEMPORARY
MONOLOGUES

1969
Tina Landau

Play
30s
Seriocomic

Mr. Martinson, teacher at Central High School, circa 1969.

When I was in high school, Class of '61—"Our life has just begun, we're the Class of '61"—my nickname was Royce the Voice, because I always did Cousin Brucie imitations—"Hey, baby, let's spin another platter and see what's the matter" . . . but my best buds called me The Raven, because I was crazy about Poe—is that redundant? Is that redundant? Now in the faculty lounge they call me "Jack Kerouac" as in "Who does he think he is?" My kids call me "Mr. Wizard," "Sid" as in Dartha, and Clark Kent, because they say when I get excited and take off my tie, I become Super-Teacher. I want to get the in-betweeners to consider college. I know the top of the class will definitely go and the bottom of the class will definitely not go—but there's that big middle group—and the bottom means Viet Nam. And the middle means Nam too. As for myself, I plan to go to finish grad school and . . . of course . . . my novel.

3 Secrets

Mike Albo and Virginia Hefferman

Original Monologue
20s+
Comic

Oh, the complexities of a grade-school romance.

In second grade I had a girlfriend during recess named
Michaellyn. She had blond hair and bright pixie blue eyes. We
were the hot couple that spring. We would walk out on the
blacktop and people would say, "Michael A. and Michaellyn!"
We were really in demand and highly visible. We spent the better part of recess walking around holding hands, making
appearances in the gravel section, visiting friends at the jungle
gym, dropping by the old dodge ball court to see the old dodge
ball gang, still single and smackin' the ball around. But I was
under such pressure. She wanted to be a horse, and she would
trot around and make me call her: "Cloudy! With a chestnut
coat, and a white star on my forehead and snout!" When we
walked through the playground she would harrumph and
clomp her feet with purebred pride. She would take me to the
part of the playground hidden by hedges and I would have to
pretend to feed her sugar cubes and carrot tops. (. . .) I didn't
mind for a while, but I just remember this time near the end of
our relationship, we were holding hands and one of the teth-
erball kids asked if we were going to get married. "Yes!
Definitely!" I heard myself say. I just stood there and smiled
and inside thought, "I am living a lie."

All Stories Are True
John Edgar Wideman

Short Story
20s-30s
Dramatic

A prisoner talks to his brother, who has come to visit.

Hey, bro, I'd be the last one to deny I'm fucked up. We both
know good and well I've had problems all my life doing what I
been supposed to do. Here I sit in this godforsaken hole if anybody needs proof I couldn't handle. Something's wrong wit me,
man, but the people who runs this joint, something's real wrong
wit them, too. (. . .)

Motherfuckers don't say shit for three months. Know I'm
on pins and needles every minute of every day since I filed my
commutation papers, but don't nobody say one god-blessed single solitary word good or bad for three months. (. . .)

Then last week I'm by the desk in the visiting room waiting
for Denise and Chance and the guard at the desk hands me the
phone, call for you. Lieutenant's on the line and he says to me
Board turned you down. Tells me I can cancel my visit and
speak to him now or check by his office later. That's it. Boom.
Turned down.

Like getting hit in the chest wit a hammer. Couldn't
breathe, man. Couldn't catch my breath for three days. Still
can't breathe right. Felt like somebody had taken a hammer
and whammed me in the heart.

All Stories Are True
John Edgar Wideman

Short Story
20s-30s
Dramatic

A prisoner tells his brother about life on the inside.

My own fault I'm in here. I know I done some bad things. I'm
in here, man, doing my time. Uh huh. Hard time. Lots of time
for doing wrong. But they treat us like dog shit in here and
that's wrong too. Guys get killed in here. Go crazy. But nobody
cares. Long as they keep us locked up they can do us anyway
they want. Figure we in here, so they don't owe us nothing. But
wrong is wrong, ain't it. Just cause we down, is it right to keep
on kicking us? Guys get meaner and crazier in here. Every day
you see the ones can't take it slipping further and further off.
Distance in their eyes, bro. Ain't nobody home in them eyes.
They shuffle around here like ghosts. Stop speaking to people.
Stop keeping theyselves clean. Gone, man. If you been around
here any length of time you seen it happen to a lot guys. You
understand how easy it is to tune out and drop off the edge
into your own little world. Another planet. You see why guys
go off. Why they so cold and mean if they ever hit the street
again.

Am I Right?
Mark Saunders

Play
28-32
Seriocomic

Sean has not had a happy day, having suffered several indignities at the hands of poor customer service, and his wife and best friend have abandoned him. After they leave, he takes stock of his day and his life.

And that was my New Year's Eve. I got badgered by a gas jockey, bullied by a restaurant manager, and obfuscated by a stupid pet store rule in a mall. The big news, of course, is my wife left me to return to Radio Free Idaho or wherever she ends up. And my best friend is getting in touch with his feminine side, after which time he will most likely leave on a jet plane for the East Coast and then move back in with his folks or, if we're all lucky, a hospital. I mean, if you can't make it here in this namby-pamby West Coast state where they won't even let you pump your own gas, you can't make it anywhere. And I mean anywhere. Am I right? Wussy state.

(. . .) But here's the thing. You think if you're married to someone, if you really love them, then you would know if they're unhappy? Am I right? And if you have a best friend who's unhappy, you should be the first one to know it. That doesn't mean you can do anything about someone else's unhappiness. Or should.

OK, maybe you should, if you can. But at the very least, you should know when the people closest to you are unhappy.

Am I right? Am I right?

Aw, what the hell.

And Now A Word from Our Sponsor

Clinton A. Johnston

Original Monologue
20+
Comic

The announcement you don't want to hear in the store you already hate.

Attention shoppers. This is your Super-Mart radio network reminding you that "We've got a lotta' great things in store." (*Drastic change in tone.*) So, buy stuff!

That's right, you heard me! Buy stuff! Move your flabby, fat asses and buy stuff! We got stuff to buy, so buy stuff! I'm not here for my health and neither are you. You're here to buy stuff! So stop dicking around and buy stuff! Hello! I don't see you buying enough stuff! We got lots of stuff here people! We got a whole store of stuff that you could be buying right now! We got items on sale. We got items at reduced prices. We got fresh, hoity-toity foods made at the deli. We've got bread baked fresh this morning. Our meat department has real meat! We've got cute little plastic crap for your kids. We've got cute, little, crappy, plastic containers for you. Get it? We've got stuff you can put stuff in! We've got seasonal stuff! We've got magazines and books. We've got stuff in the aisles, stuff on top of the aisles, stuff at the checkout stand! Hey! Things are stuff all over! Buy more stuff! Buy stuff! Buy stuff! Buy stuff!

Angels in America
Tony Kushner

Play
30s
Dramatic

Belize differs with Louis on the subject of patriotism.

You know what your problem is, Louis? Your problem is that you are so full of piping hot crap that the mention of your name draws flies.

Up in the air, just like that angel, too far off the earth to pick out the details. Louis and his Big Ideas. Big Ideas are all you love. "America" is what Louis loves. Well I hate America, Louis. I hate this country. It's just big ideas, and stories, and people dying, and people like you.

The cracker who wrote the national anthem knew what he was doing. He set the word "free" to a note so high nobody can reach it. That was deliberate. Nothing on earth sounds less like freedom to me.

You come with me to room 1013 over at the hospital, I'll show you America. Terminal, crazy, and mean.

I live in America, Louis, that's hard enough. I don't have to love it. You do that. Everybody's got to love something.

Angels in America
Tony Kushner

Play
30s
Dramatic

Joe, a clean-cut Mormon lawyer, crumbles under the pressure of convention. He sits outside the Courts building.

Um . . . Yesterday was Sunday . . . but I've been a little unfocused recently, and I thought it was Monday. So I came here like I was going to work. And the whole place was empty. And at first I couldn't figure out why, and I had this moment of incredible . . . fear and also . . . It just flashed through my mind: The whole Hall of Justice, it's empty, it's deserted, it's gone out of business. Forever. The people that make it run have up and abandoned it. I felt that I was going to scream. Not because it was creepy, but because the emptiness felt so fast. And well . . . good . . . A happy scream. I just wondered what a thing it would be . . . if overnight everything you owe anything to . . . justice, or love, had really gone away. Free. It would be . . . heartless terror. Yes. Terrible and . . . Very great. To shed your skin, every old skin, one by one and then walk unencumbered into the morning. *(Little pause. He looks at the building.)* I can't go in there today.

Angels in America

Tony Kushner

Play
30+
Seriocomic

*Louis is wracked with guilt for not having the strength to care
for his AIDS-stricken partner.*

You're a nurse! Give me something! I . . . don't know what to
do anymore, I . . . Last week at work I screwed up the Xerox
machine like permanently, and so I . . . then I tripped on the
subway steps and my glasses broke and I cut my forehead, here,
see, and now I can't see much and my forehead, it's like the
Mark of Cain, stupid, right, but it won't heal and every morning I see and I think, Biblical things, Mark of Cain, Judas
Iscariot and his silver and his noose, people who . . . in betray-
ing what they love betray what's truest in themselves, I feel . . .
nothing but cold for myself, just cold, and every night I miss
him, I miss him so much but then . . . those sores, and the
smell, and . . . where I thought it was going . . . I could be . . . I
could be sick too, maybe I'm sick too, I don't know . . .

Belize . . . Tell him I love him. Can you do that? (*LOUIS
puts his head in his hands, inadvertently touching his cut forehead.*) OW!!!!!! DAMN!

Anger Box
Jeff Goode

Original Monologue
35+
Dramatic

On hearing that a gas station owner's murder is being called a "hate crime," a "good upstanding American" launches into a diatribe on Justice.

You don't know what he was like, this guy.

I mean, this guy . . . No disrespect, but just between you and me.

Thank God. OK? Good riddance. There I said it.

And I know how that makes me look, but sometimes you gotta just stand up for your rights and say, I don't care what anybody thinks, that's just how it is. And if you disagree, I'm sorry, but you don't know.

Because that's the thing is you'll have people from all over, from New York, or fucking San Francisco, writin' about . . . I don't know. *Intolerance.* Or, I don't know, *profiling.* Because of how something looks on the surface, but do they even take the time to come down here and find out, or research or even ask somebody? Do they ask anybody? (. . .)

Like, for example, this guy who got shot.

Fine upstanding business owner, member of the community, right?

But where did he get the money to own a business?

Just over from what-the-fuck. Two years in this country, five years, I dunno, whatever. (. . .) Five years maybe, tops.

Hasn't even learned the language and then—boom—owns his own business.

Like I'm buying that. Bullshit.

I've been fifteen years on my job and I don't own shit. I'm still paying for my truck.

(. . .)Being an American don't count for shit in this country.

Angry Young Man

Daniel Trujillo

Play
20s
Comic

Frank, a hyperprincipled, anticommercial stage director, berates his friend Phil for his conversation with a theater big-shot, Barry Corman.

The two of us were out on Houston Street
And who, of all Manhattan, should we meet,
The grossest pig to don an author's cap
And punish us by publishing his crap!
Yeah! Barry Corman asks to use your lighter!
But then, instead of saying he's not a writer,
And that you're sick of life-affirming comedies,
And it's a crime his plays are Tony nominees,
You say to him, "I've always liked your stuff."
What fluffernutter! God, I've had enough.
Nobody wants to tell the truth these days.
That doesn't mean I'm going to stoop to praise
A rotten playwright's simpleminded dirt
To guarantee their feelings don't get hurt.
An artist needs to hear what people think,
And when they lay one, someone smells the stink.
I hate this whole politically correct
Infection. All of it is false respect
And artificial sweetener. Follow me?
You saccharin of mediocrity?
A guy who wouldn't voice a critical word

Isn't the theater's ally. He's absurd.
He's lacking taste. His whole opinion's jack.
Can't tell the worthy talent from the hack.
So I can't trust you, Patron of the Arts.
Your praise comes just as easily as your farts.

Any Suspicious Activity
Roger Nieboer

Play
20+
Seriocomic

A lonely executive begins a gradual descent into international marketing hell.

I'm sitting in the office. Late at night. I'm the only one here. Everyone else has gone home, or wherever it is they go when they leave the office. It's very quiet and very still. I'm trying to finish up some last minute . . . details, on the presentation I'm scheduled to give tomorrow, to an important delegation. Somewhere. In Cleveland, or Hong Kong, or . . . Berlin . . . I can't remember where, exactly. I'll have to check the itinerary. It doesn't really seem to matter. The presentation will undoubtedly take place in the conference room of a major hotel. It will look and feel like any conference room in any major hotel in any city anywhere. There will be chilled plastic bottles of purified water waiting at every table. There will be pens and pads of paper conveniently placed. There will be outlets, jacks, adaptors, and fiber-optic cables capable of connecting me to any communications system anywhere. But I still need to come up with a decent conclusion, to wrap it all up, tie it together, drop it in their laps . . . but I can't. I'm stuck; I'm in a rut. I'm drawing a total immaculately conceptual blank. I have turned off the lights, closed the door, and am leaning comfortably back in my chair, but I am frozen with fear. I just don't know what to do. Jump? Shout? Run? Scream? All these options and more flash through my cortex in a blaze of possible neurological responses.

Then I feel it, the pin-prickling of claws across the back of my right hand. Before I can respond, the creature scurries up my arm and is gone. I sit transfixed, in my chair, before rising slowly to turn on the lights.

The Apocryphal Transcripts of Clear Eddie

John Colburn

Original Monologue
40s
Dramatic

The speaker is a street character, called by some an "acid casualty."

The truth is, friend, our lives are guided
by unanswerable questions.
Answers lack.
It's how the questions expand our world
that's important.
Yesterday I had a court date
a simple consequence
of speaking in the language of desire and not fear
which our society happens to hate
but to me it all seemed like a beautiful play
a highly ritualized aesthetic experience
I told the judge that
I said "this is a highly ritualized aesthetic experience
and I appreciate it, your honor"
and behind his official expression of annoyance
which keeps him in character
I saw the flicker of another expression—
pleasure or approval or satisfaction.
Then the judge told me a story
of my hypothetical life.
In his story

I was naked again
—this sounds like a dream, doesn't it,
a dream the judge is having for me—
anyway I was naked again
and holding my sign again
and the police came again
only this time they
were even less kind
they locked me up
and the judge believed at the end of this
hypothetical "incarceration"
I would understand time.
It was a beautiful performance
a vision
the state paid someone to create
like paying a novelist to come to my house
and depict one possible future.
The judge asked me not to repeat my mistakes;
I told the judge repetition gives life structure.

The Art Machine

Adam Szymkowicz

Play
Late teens
Dramatic

The Boy is autistic, an inventor, and possibly a mechanical genius. He is describing a new invention, which is getting clearer in his mind. Soon he will be able to build.

It's coming. Very soon, it's coming. I can feel it gripping my neck, working its way into my voice. Drying up the dust, flooding through. It's getting clearer. Certain parts I see very well. But I still don't have the whole of it. Under my skin, running around my brain, electric gerbils building tracks, connecting, connecting, building and connecting. Coursing through my cortex, one and then two and then stopping and building more track so the train can get through, so this huge thing I don't know what it is yet can get through. So this huge . . . don't ask me questions. I won't answer you because I'm not really here. I'm in a place there's no words for and even if I had the words, I wouldn't tell you. I wouldn't tell you because you would never understand. I'm not like you. I can't . . . don't want to operate. I just know how things should go. And let me tell you a secret. This thing, this thing that's coming is going to dwarf the old one. But not yet. Not yet. It's coming. I'll tell you when it's here, but not yet. For now, let them believe what they want. I'm a void, an empt . . . these words are painful. Don't ask me anymore. I'm not talking anymore.

Balm in Gilead
Lanford Wilson

Play
35+
Comic

The endurance of cockroaches blows a heroin-addict's mind.

A roach's attitude just gripes the hell out of me. But what burns
me, I've been reading up not recently, but I saw it somewhere
where . . . (. . .) anthropologists or whatever, *geologists* over
in Egypt or somewhere, looking for the first city, they dug
down through a city, and straight on down through another,
you know, they're piled up like a sandwich or in layers like a
seven-layer cake. And they cut down, down through one
century to the one before it and the one before that, and in
every one they found more goddamned cockroaches than
anything! And they got to where before man ever existed and,
like, in the basement of the whole works, there those damn
bugs still were.
 So they've been around, like I said, for about a million
years before we came along. But not only that! They've made
tests, and they found out that a roach can stand—if there was
going to be a big atom bomb explosion, they can stand something like fourteen times as much radio-whatever-it-is, you-
know-*activity* as we can. So after every man, woman and child
is wiped out and gone, like you imagine, those same goddamn
cockroaches will still be crawling around happy as you please
over the ruins of everything.
 Now the picture of that really gripes my ass!

Bang
Neal Lerner

Play
30-35
Comic

*Bill—charming, good-natured, urban-neurotic—is an almost-
successful actor. Late one evening he sits up in bed and
recounts to Guy his exhausting morning routine.*

So anyway, I watch the news, which you know I love. Sort of
jump-starts my day. I pack up my things—gym stuff, Zone bar,
all my things, you know—and get my sorry self to Crunch. I'm
a little oodgy because I get to the subway just as the train is
arriving, which leaves me no time to walk down the platform
to the back of the train, which means when I get off at 42nd
Street, I have to trudge much further through the hot and stink
to use the 40th Street exit, which is worth it because it leaves
me out at Broadway, which means I then only have to walk
two blocks south to Crunch. So, I'm feeling behind already
time-wise. I'm walking in the front door and I'm mentally
checking to make sure I have my membership ID number ready
by heart—pthoo2768. How un-catchy and hard to recall every
morning is that?! I've always resented my membership ID number. Seems unfair and difficult to me. I wonder if everyone's
pass number is so unrecognizable—or did I just get unlucky
when I joined, or maybe did the person who signed me up not
like me because I'm gay or because I have a hair system on my
head, or maybe he thinks I'm just too old to be at the joining
stage. Their motto is "No Judgments" and yet I often, so often

I tell you feel judged. Those pumped up trainers look right through me which pisses me off—saddens me too though—for them I mean—anyway, so I remember my number but it's always a somewhat tense moment for me.

Bang
Neal Lerner

Play
30-35
Seriocomic

Charming, good-natured, urban-neurotic Bill describes his "fat child" past to his new friend.

There was a particularly carefree afternoon, and I was sort of exploring the different parts of my yard—(. . .) I guess the adult term for this is imagination—my mom's term for this was goofing off. (. . .) I spy something new on the lawn. I walk over and pick it up—all shiny, with a pretty green and white label. It's a can of DelMonte Green Peas, the kind I like, the dark green mushy ones, not the horrible Kelly green ones that are kind of hard and dry. The can is half open. I don't know what comes over me, but I become obsessed. I have to have these peas. I found them, they are mine, my peas. I grab the can and hide with it under our big evergreen tree, truly a horrible place to try and sit, especially with shorts on, with all the evergreen needles pressing into my thighs and my tushie. Well, but, so then, like some sort of half-crazed, starving savage, I push my hand down into the can and grab some of those peas. I've done it. My hand is now stuck in the can. (. . .) Well, this is a fresh hell, my worst nightmare come true before my eyes. Selma is definitely going to kill me for this. I mean, I'd pushed her pretty far in the past, I mean, my being a fat child had brought her enough shame over those early years. This was grounds for severe repercussions. How pathetic and embarrassing can you get—her fat child, getting stuck in a half-opened can of DelMonte Peas that has fallen out of the neighbors' garbage, probably seen by the neighbors, and in-between meals!

The Beauty and Terror
of Being a Dog

Steven Schutzman

Play
Mid-20s
Seriocomic

Maze has been laid up with a leg injury, going stir-crazy. Denied his kinetic ways, he confronts questions he usually avoids about himself and his life.

Chicago's where I'm going all right. I always wanted to live in Chicago because it's what you do there that counts. What you actually do. If you do nothing you do nothing and nobody asks about the goddamn philosophy behind it. I'll get a job with the railroad or I'll work in a meat locker or I'll operate a grain elevator. Yeah I'll be a grain elevator operator. And I'll marry a black woman who can sing. Or maybe she can't sing a note. It won't matter because we'll be living real life in a real place with real, no-bullshit Chicago people around us. I could stand being around some people who are a little less "interesting" than you are, Aaron. And it'll be freezing cold in the winter. I'll go into the meat locker to get warm in the winter. And it'll be goddamn hotter than hell in the summer. Not like California where you can't tell the season without looking for the date on the newspaper. This place gets on my nerves. People like you lying around depressed in the dark get on my nerves. Ruthie gets on my nerves with all her talk about people being together but separate and everyone working to transform himself all the time. I don't want to be transformed. What's wrong with me the way I am? If she doesn't want me the way I am then to hell with her.

You know what she told me? She said she was in love with what I could become, what I could become when I changed like she knew I would change. Can you believe that? A black woman would never say that to her man.

Better Places to Go
David-Matthew Barnes

Play
Early 20s
Seriocomic

Derek, suicidal and manic, harbors feelings of unrequited love for his best friend, Ricardo.

It's killing me. Not being able to be with you. I'd rather let them shoot me dead and murder me than to go another day of my life without being with you. I know you're mad at me because you wanted us to wait a little bit before we finally left. But I can't wait anymore. I swear to God, I'll die. I hate this place. I hate everyone here because they all hate me. And I don't ever want them to hate you. So if we leave tonight, we can get away from here before they turn on you like they've turned against me. And I'll be good in California. I promise. I'll take the medication and I'll try to stop the noise in my head, once and for all. And I'll work really hard and I'll do whatever I have to do. But if we stay here, I'll die. My heart can't take it no more, Ricardo. I lay awake at night and I listen to Britney and Nathan beat the hell out of each other and I close my eyes and I pretend that you're there with me and you're holding me and I feel safe and I feel loved and that's all I've ever wanted. Please. Let's go. Tonight. If we do, I know I'll still be alive when dawn breaks.

The Blacks: A Clown Show
Jean Genet
Translated by Bernard Frechtman

Play
20+
Dramatic

A group of black players enacts the ritualistic murder of a white woman before a jury of white-masked blacks, then they condemn the court itself. Shocking for its time, the play still holds up for its violent attack against the society and privilege of the white race. Here, a player named Village kneels before Virtue, a black woman.

When I beheld you, you were walking in the rain, in high heels. (. . .) Oh, if only I hadn't been flooded with a strange emotion, but we—you and I were moving along the edges of the world, out of bounds. (. . .) I was unable to bear the weight of the world's condemnation. And I began to hate you when everything about you would have kindled my love and when love would have made men's contempt unbearable, and their contempt would have made my love unbearable. The fact is, I hate you. (. . .)

I know not whether you are beautiful. I fear you may be. I fear your sparkling darkness. Oh darkness, stately mother of my race, shadow, sheath that swathes me from top to toe, long sleep in which the frailest of your children would love to be shrouded, I know not whether you are beautiful, but you are Africa, oh monumental night, and I hate you. I hate you for filling my black eyes with sweetness. I hate you for making me thrust you from me, for making me hate you. It would take so little for your face, your body, your movements, your heart to thrill me (. . .). But I hate you!

The Blacks: A Clown Show
Jean Genet
Translated by Bernard Frechtman

Play
20+
Dramatic

A group of black players enacts the ritualistic murder of a white woman before a jury of white-masked blacks, then they condemn the court itself. Shocking for its time, the play still holds up for its violent attack against the society and privilege of the white race. Here, a player named Archibald makes a grave entreaty.

I order you to be black to your very veins. Pump black blood through them. Let Africa circulate in them. Let Negroes negrify themselves. Let them persist to the point of madness in what they're condemned to be, in their ebony, in their odor, in their yellow eyes, in their cannibal tastes. Let them not be content with eating Whites, but let them cook each other as well. Let them invent recipes for shinbones, kneecaps, calves, thick lips, everything. Let them invent unknown sauces. Let them invent hiccoughs, belches and farts that'll give out a deleterious jazz. Let them invent a criminal painting and dancing. Negroes, if they change toward us, let it not be out of indulgence, but terror.

Blade to the Heat
Oliver Mayer

Play
20s+
Dramatic

Wilfred Vinal accuses his boxing ring opponents of homosexuality, which usually rattles them to disadvantage. When his trainer tells him to cool it, Vinal defends himself.

You come to a stinky gym like this for a reason. It's always something. Some assholes they just like to fight. Other guys they got to prove something. The little ones they got a complex. Big ones they got a complex too. Some of these clowns like to beat on other guys to impress the chicks, like it'll make their dick bigger or something. Then there's the other kind. They here 'cause they like the smell of men. They like to share sweat. They like the form, man. The way a dude looks when he throws a blow, his muscles all strained and sweaty, his ass all tight bearing down on the blow, his mouth all stopped up with a piece of rubber, and only a pair of soaking wet trunks between his johnson and yours. They like it. And they like to catch a whupping for liking it. That's just the way it is. I'm surprised man. Thought you knew the business, old-timer.

Bodhisattva by Lagoon

Cass Brayton

Play
30s-40s
Dramatic

A drag queen manages her man.

"Are you ashamed of me?" I asked?
It's the only time I saw him flustered.
I didn't bring it up at the time it happened,
Which was not long after
We first made our acquaintance.
We were on an evening promenade,
Taking in the sights out on the street.
Just talking, you know,
Getting to know each other,
Feeling each other out.
One of his friends runs into us.
Literally runs into us.
He comes barreling out of a store
Guzzling a drink of some kind
—you know—oblivious.
Slams right into us.
He's someone I'd seen around.
Kinda cute, kinda dumb.
Always an appealing combination.
I elbowed Sprout.
"Introduce your friend."
So he did.
Then we continued on
But I could tell he kind of blushed,

Embarrassed that the oblivious guy
Saw the two of us together.
A few days later,
When we were fighting about something
I brought it up.
He denied it, but I called him on it.
'Cause it's one thing a queen can just feel,
like a waitress knows a tipper,
like a hooker knows a cop,
like a cheerleader knows the score.
He copped to it,
Said he'd felt like he was
Introducing his mother.
At least I didn't remind him of his father.
He said he'd never treat me
That way again.
Promise.
I like the way contrition
Can turn someone into a little cherub.
So I blew out the candle
And let him make it up to me.

Bronx
Danny Hoch

Play
20s
Dramatic

A man loiters in a hallway of the C-74 building on Riker's Island, New York City. He converses with a new inmate.

See, I try to do the right thing, they lock me up. Giuliani's like, "Oh, people on welfare are lazy." I'm trying not to be on that shit. I'm workin', right? I'm in Fordham Road. I'm sellin' Bart Simpson T-shirts, and um, what you call it—O. J. Simpson T-shirts, right? This cop come up, arrest me 'cause I don't got a license. (. . .)

You know, I'm tryin' to do right in my life, man. I wanna be a entrepreneur, or whatever you call it. You know if I was that little girl that they show on TV in that commercial selling lemonade in front of her house, you think the cop gonna arrest *her*? Nah-ah! Nah-ah! (. . .)

See, if you analyze it with the little girl and the lemonade, that's supposed to be America, right? That you could stand outside your house and sell whatever. If that's not true that you could do that, don't advertise it then. Don't put it in the TV, you know? To be honest with you, I seen that commercial, I got inspired by that shit. I said yo, shit ain't really that bad, I got chances and shit. Now I'm in fucking jail, bro. I feel like *suing* them lemonade motherfuckers, man. Or suing somebody . . . For false advertising . . . I know I wasn't selling lemonade, that's not the—Hey yo, shut up, bro. I didn't really ask you to respond and shit, damn.

Brown Hearts Bleed Young

W. Brandon Lacy Campos

Original Monologue
23
Dramatic

Rada, a gay Latino, speaks at a community center where other youth have gathered to talk about violence. He has a slight barrio accent.

Violence has affected every one of us. We are young, we are brown, we are Latino, we are queer, we are intimately aware of violence in every step we've ever taken in our lives. Our bodies have been marked by the violence of what it means to not be white in this country. Violence is turning on the television and only seeing us as convicts, criminals, drug addicts, and domestic servants. It is English-only laws, California Propositions, dead trannies in Colorado, and Border Patrol bullets. It is hearing our language commodified, our music appropriated, our history co-opted in a new wave minstrel show where "brown face" is in as long as the only way it enters your house is on the Latin Grammy's. I know violence intimately. The brutality bred by necessity and survival and the violence born of HIV in this body. Violence is believing that I was going to contract this virus no matter what, so I said fuck it and got fucked.

The Burning
Duncan Ley

Play
Dramatic
20s

Francis Schiller, the Bishop's son, recalls his wife's execution.

I said my name would protect her. (*He pauses and turns to his father.*) I said to Madeline our name would protect her. (*PHILIPP cannot continue looking at FRANCIS.*) They burned three witches that day. They led me out in chains to watch. At first I could not recognize her. She was bruised, they all were bruised and bloodied, and they stared into the crowd with these vacant eyes. She looked right at me but I could tell she never saw me. I thought that maybe my presence would lessen the ordeal. I was wrong. As I watched her burn I hummed a little tune that Madeline used to sing to me. She would cradle me in her arms and rub my forehead and sing gently. So I sang it for her. But she would not have heard it. I thought she would still have the grace to die honourably, as a martyr to all that had been wrought against her. But there was no honour in her death. She wailed as the flames leapt up, and as her skin began to blacken from the heat her wail became this scream, then the scream became a gargle, and I believe then she died. (. . .) My last memory of Madeline is her burning. Whenever I close my eyes and try to remember her that is all I see.

Business Casual
Adam Hahn

Original Monologue
22+
Comic

A co-worker takes a flirtatious joke too far.

There's a girl in the cubicle next to mine. (. . .)

I was eating lunch at my desk a couple of weeks ago when she came in, grabbed my granola bar (. . .), and ran out. Then I heard her giggling in her cubicle, (. . .) "Now it's my granola bar!"

Since then, we've been stealing things as a way of flirting with each other. We'll take each other's pens, or on Friday I ran away with her mouse pad, saying I was "King of the Mouse pads!" (. . .)

I had this great idea. She's diabetic, and every day she gives herself a shot after lunch. (. . .) [T]his morning, I snuck over, and I took her syringe and the insulin out of her purse. (. . .)

I'm going to jump up when she gets back and say, "Who is the Wizard of Glucose Regulation? With this magic wand, with this magic potion, I must be the Wizard of Glucose Regulation!"

I wonder where she is. It's almost time to go home, and she hasn't come back from lunch yet. What happened to her?

If I can pry off the panel where the wiring goes beneath through the cubicle divider, I want to try to steal one of her shoes while she's typing.

Can You Tell Me How to Get (fill in the blank)?

Luke Pingel

Original Monologue
20s+
Comic

Some guys are just not cut out for the kiddie entertainment industry.

My name is Tad. People my whole life have told me how rough around the edges I am. They say I'm abrasive or some shit like that. I dunno, I've never been able to figure it out. I am a nice guy. I have a good heart. I love children. Yeah! I love children! And what do people do when I tell them I love children? Just nod and change the subject. What? Like I'm too rough around the edges to love children? I tell those people to fuck off.

I've dedicated my entire life to children, touring with Sesame Street on Ice for nine years now. I auditioned for Big Bird, but they started saying all that shit about being too abrasive or rough around the edges, and I told them to fuck off. They offered me a job on electrics crew, and I told them to fuck off, but I took the job anyway. I think it's my thick beard that makes me seem abrasive or rough around the edges. Yeah, I tried to saw off Snuffy's nose with my skate? So what? You don't think Big Bird gets tired of his shit sometimes?

But I do what I do for the children. If I can be a part of something that can make those fuckers smile, I am a happy Tad.

Charlie's Bird Store
Richard Davis, Jr.

Play
50s
Dramatic

A war veteran recalls a defining moment.

I was flying with the Vietnamese . . . in a chopper. They had
these two guys they thought were Viet Cong, and we were supposed to interrogate them. We were flying at 750 feet. I could
see the ground real clear. Trees blowing in the wind, goats in a
field. Looking down at 750 feet is scarier than looking down at
30,000 feet because at 30,000, nothing looks real. We hovered
while the interrogators chirped away, while the Viet Cong
dudes sat there, staring at the floor. One of the interrogators
slid the door open. The wind rushed in cold and loud. The
other interrogator grabbed the nearest guy and . . . threw him
out. Guy didn't have time to yell. He looked at me while he
was in the air, and for that tiny second, he looked like someone
who gets pushed into a swimming pool . . . arms and legs
swirling. It was almost funny. He tried to grab at the chopper,
but he couldn't. And I felt like some vacuum, something in his
eyes, was pulling me out after him . . . I thought maybe it's a
trick, maybe they had put a rope on him . . . but he . . . hit the
ground. Goats scattered . . . . He had gotten himself in exactly
the wrong situation. And there was nothing he could do about
it. No planning, no begging . . . because he was already in the
situation. And he didn't have wings.

Christmas Spirit
Daniel Drennan

Essay
20s+
Comic

*Holiday pressure to end the "should we get a tree?" argument
has the narrator bah-humbugging all over New York.*

I know that he wants a tree to decorate, and so last night I
decided to go out and get a tree and surprise him, my own
pathetically warped version of an O. Henry story. (. . .)
The temperature was below freezing outside as I headed down
Columbus Avenue, and I passed one of the huge tree stands set
up on the sidewalk that blocks all pedestrian traffic (. . .).

   The farther I walk the more I notice that there seems to be
more needles on the ground than on the trees themselves. I
cross over to Broadway and there is another tree stand and
some Nova Scotia lady asks if she can help me and she starts
doing that bang-the-tree tree-banging gesture to show that the
needles are fast on the trees she is displaying, and I ask the
price since I had about thirty-five bucks in my pocket and she
was like, "Forty-five" and I was like, "What kind of tree will
thirty-five dollars get me?" at which point she glances over at
the Charlie Brown section. I don't even know why they bother
to cut down these pathetic scrawny saplings, which are basical-
ly the forested version of tiny fish stupid enough to get caught
in tuna nets.

   At this point I have decided: I hate Christmas, I hate New
York, I hate Nova Scotia, I hate everything and everyone; but I
trudge home and get some more money and return and buy the

nice tree from the Nova Scotia lady and carry it home to surprise the now-happy boyfriend which makes me happy in turn until I read in today's *Times* that the City is Grinch-like reviving a fire code law in New York that forbids live trees in New York City residences. And I can't sleep for thinking about the leaping flames of Christmas cheer that we might end up spreading throughout my entire apartment building.

Church of the Open Mind
Allyson Currin

Play
30s
Seriocomic

*Gid, a young doctor, is faced with the return of his frustrating
ex-fiancé, Cassie, who has just written a searing failed novel
about her searing failed relationship with Gid. So now it's time
for Gid to let Cassie have it.*

Hear that? That, my love, is silence.

We get a lot of it around these parts. We're fond of it.
Sometimes we even get a wild hair up our ass and break it. But
mostly we just listen to it.

You didn't hear it because you're not trained to listen. A
part of that vast education that was totally ignored. Your father
has convinced you that every word you utter is a pearl, which
BY RIGHT should be shared with the general public. So you've
ended up a mixed-up kid who substitutes volume for substance.
You want to know the real reason your precious book got
panned?

People finally figured out that you're nothing but a charming babbler. The worst kind, too. And you'll remain a charming
babbler until you learn to listen to other people.

You've fallen on your ass, big deal. As I see it, you've got
two choices. Want to hear them? You can either stop writing
charming babble. Or you can stop talking to listen to other
people around you who are DYING to talk for a change. You
might hear a few things that surprise you.

You want to tell the truth? Fine, go to it, Godspeed.

But make goddamn sure you're hearing it straight before
you write it down.

Circle A
Cathy Camper

Novel
16
Dramatic

Jack and Marnie are on the high school swim team. Marnie is hanging out with punks, wants to quit the team, and breaks up with Jack. Here, Jack offers some advice.

You know, I didn't always used to like to swim. (. . .) When I was a little kid, my parents sent me to summer camp every year. And every year I was the only black kid, and these other kids would gang up on me and hold me underwater so I couldn't breathe. And I'd try to tell the counselors but they'd ignore me. So I became terrified of the water. It took me years to get over that. And sometimes even now when I first put my face down into the pool I can feel that fear . . . it still rises up in my throat like it's gonna choke me. And I get so fuckin' angry; I'm never gonna let anyone stop me like that again! Only I'm afraid that this time it's gonna be you Marnie they're holding down, and you're not gonna know it until it's too late and you drown. Do you really think when they're onto the next thing they're gonna give a shit what happens to you?

Cities of the Mountain
Jim Cowen

Play
35
Dramatic

It's 1952, during the Korean War and McCarthy Era. Ross Montana has just suggested a strategy for avoiding service in the army to a client, Murtha, a twenty-two-year-old. It entailed faking a suicide and undergoing a ten-day observation at Bellevue's Psycho Ward. Fascinated at the prospect of a stint in the nuthouse, Murtha has implored Ross to draw him a picture of what to expect if one were to be "thrown into the violent ward."

Everybody should be in the nuthouse. Once at least. Gives you a little perspective on the outside world. You take the average man who's well adjusted . . . put him in the Violent Ward for twenty-four hours, if he comes out of there with his sanity intact, it's gonna be a miracle! You've got to have an iron clad constitution for that boy! I took it for twenty-four hours. And I survived by the skin of my teeth. Patty the safecracker's the only other guy I ever saw do it. He took it for two weeks! Shook up alright—but he came out of it in one piece. On his first day out he played me a game of checkers in the sun room. And beat me! Hah! Rare case! Anybody else, twenty-four hours push you right over the edge! (*He continues with a tough, hard edge, sinister threat in his voice.*)

You get out there boy! Hah-hahhhh! That's a long journey back. Most of them never make it. Take my word. I've seen them break. You got so much as one screw loose, you'll crack in that environment. That's a screaming, howling hell over there! I've seen them—stranded out there—screaming for help.

Closure
Steve Martin

Essay
20s+
Comic

A man is a teensy bit obsessive about his need for closure.

Closure. I wanted it. Or I wasn't going to be able to move on. (. . .)

My movie theater free admission coupon is not being honored. A line forms behind me as I explain my situation to the ticket seller. I had called ahead to make sure it would be honored. They said it would be. Yet here I am, being embarrassed in front of strangers. Josie says, "Let's pay," and suggests that we move on. I cannot. I tell them I will need closure. The man selling tickets says the coupon people made the mistake, and they are the ones who will need to take responsibility. "So you need closure," I say. "Yes," he replies, "before we can move on." "So my closure is dependent on your closure," I say. "Yes." Just then Josie says, "I need closure too, tonight." She pays. I move on, even though I am unable to move on.

We watch the movie. It is about Mary Queen of Scots. She was beheaded. At least she got closure.

Coercion

Katie Leo

Play
40s-50s
Dramatic

Dale is a working-class white male, speaking to his adopted Korean daughter, Kim. Throughout the monologue, Dale drinks scotch. Kim's adoptive mother, Brenda, is also in the room.

You came over on a plane with forty other Korean orphans. It was a huge jumbo jet full of babies. Biggest load of foreign babies we'd ever seen. The paper called it a "jet stork." Your mother was so nervous, she packed up this duffel bag full of baby crap—diapers, wipes, powder, toys, three changes of clothing—you name it. I mean, a kid coulda lived off that bag for months!

(. . .) We felt like angels were watching over us that night. But nothing could compare with when we saw you.

So, all these ladies came off the plane with babies in their hands. I'd never seen so many dark-skinned kids, and all with full heads of hair. I mean it . . . you all had this thick, black hair! Then they started calling off numbers and names. And your mother and I are standing there, watching everyone around us meeting their kids. And, we're thinking, "When's it gonna be our turn? What if there was a mistake?" But, finally we heard our number.

You were perfect, Kim. All those months of trying—the tests, the questions, the pressure, everyone asking, "When? When?"—all that pain was worth it. And, that bitch social worker, Mrs. Lathrop, who didn't believe in white people raising an Oriental—even suffering through that biddy's endless questions was worth it.

Concerned Catholics

Barbara Lhota and Janet B. Milstein

Play
40s
Dramatic

Father Thomas confronts Gretchen, his assistant and good friend for many years, who has joined with several parishioners to expose gay priests. This group of "Concerned Catholics" are on the warpath to eliminate gay priests from the churches, because they feel this will prevent further sexual abuse cases.

Of course I realize that! So blame the people who put the priests back into positions and exposed the children again. Blame the priesthood for being tight-knit and stubborn and stupid as hell, but do not blame gay men in the priesthood. Not all gay men—just like not all heterosexual men—abuse children. I hope you realize that! I can't believe you're targeting them! What you're suggesting, Gretchen, is just a huge witch hunt to me—no different than rooting out communists or even the Jews. For the gay priests who have done quiet duty for years at parishes never harming anyone and, in fact, making the lives of the people there much better—would you go after them too? *(She nods.)* What did they do wrong? Gay priests have been speaking to their parish and advising for more than a hundred years. Despite all our denial, they have served the elderly, brought food to the bake sale and gave your children first communion. This witch hunt may not kill the Catholic Church, but it'll do serious damage. If you want to do something, create a support group for the survivors or demand more action if abuse occurs in the future. Anything, except try to rid the church of us. *(Beat.)* Yes . . . us.

Confessions of a Recovering Teenager

Jonathan Dorf

Play
Teens
Seriocomic

Jude has just been released from a psychiatric hospital—he had tried to kill himself.

I bet my real father is an alcoholic. And a criminal. A really psychotic criminal who killed his entire family and then went to the Super Fresh to get Florida oranges on sale. And not just on sale. He had coupons. Double coupons. And a manufacturer's rebate. And he got into a shootout at the cash register when they didn't want to give him the double discount. *(Beat.)*

It would explain a lot. *(Beat.)*

When I think what my real mom is like, I draw a blank. I close my eyes, and I try to picture her. I see Madonna, a half-dozen different supermodels, you know like from the *Sports Illustrated* swimsuit issue. The usual. The perfect mom. And she vacuums the living room in tight shorts. My mom can wear tight denim shorts. She cooks in her swimsuit, and the food tastes good too. *(Beat.)*

But then the weird stuff starts. My mom, she changes. Suddenly, she's some lady in armor burning at the stake, or that crazy woman in the movie who keeps screaming "No wire hangers." Or the Greek chick with all the snakes in her hair, and if you look at her you turn to stone. And I look at her. Into her eyes. Suddenly I can't breathe, and it's like my muscles are getting tight, and I try to move and I can't. I'm turning to stone.

Crush Everlasting
Dave Ulrich

Monologue
20s-30s
Comic

A very fast-talking, obsessive young man realizes they call it a "crush" for a reason.

Ah. I met this girl. First things, first. You know. I'm at the post office. Standing in line. Quick assessment. Scan the room. There. Ass. Nice ass. Very, very nice ass. That's it. Big deal. And turn. Profile. Good. Very good. And I start trying to see the rest. Slight moves, angles, willpower: "Turn around. Turn around. Turn around." Subliminal. And at last. The turn. Brief, but telling, and . . . Oh my god. Bah boom, bah boom. Oh my god. That . . . I could look into those eyes endlessly. I'm certain. Immediately, I'm certain. I want to know what's in there. I want to learn from her. I want to teach her. I want to share, to know. Oh—my—god.

Here's the crazy thing. Here's the thing that doesn't happen. She looks, take me in, and she smiles. That doesn't happen. That doesn't happen with . . . or when . . . you know, I want—

The crush. Ah, the crush. You know the crush. The blood quickens and thins. The heat enveloping the head from the temples. Short breaths, ears tingling, throat tightens, limbs limp, feet numb, and balance suddenly conscious. Instant crush. This woman—This—woman . . . is all the more remarkable to me because I don't begin with hurdles, I don't just beg for her eyes, her attention—she gave them. She gave to me. Just gave them. Who does that? Who does that, that looks like her? To a guy like me? Who?

The Curious Incident of the Dog in the Night-Time

Mark Haddon

Novel

15

Dramatic

Christopher is a mathematically gifted, autistic fifteen-year-old who discovers a neighborhood dog murdered.

The dog was dead. There was a garden fork sticking out of the dog. The points of the fork must have gone all the way through the dog and into the ground because the fork had not fallen over. I decided that the dog was probably killed with the fork because I could not see any other wounds in the dog and I do not think you would stick a garden fork into a dog after it had died for some other reason, like cancer, for example, or a road accident. But I could not be certain about this. (. . .)

My name is Christopher John Francis Boone. I know all the countries of the world and their capital cities and every prime number up to 7,057. (. . .)

I like dogs. You always know what a dog is thinking. It has four moods. Happy, sad, cross and concentrating. Also, dogs are faithful and they do not tell lies because they cannot talk. (. . .)

I looked up and saw Mrs. Shears running toward me from the patio. (. . .) She was shouting, "What in fuck's name have you done to my dog?"

I do not like people shouting at me. It makes me scared that they are going to hit me or touch me and I do not know what is going to happen. (. . .) I put my hands over my ears and closed my eyes and rolled forward till I was hunched up with my forehead pressed onto the grass. The grass was wet and cold. It was nice.

The Curious Incident of the Dog in the Night-Time

Mark Haddon

Novel
35+
Dramatic

A father explains to his autistic son his relationship with a neighbor.

Please. Christopher. Just . . . let me explain. (. . .) When your mum left . . . Eileen . . . Mrs. Shears . . . she was very good to us. Very good to me. She helped me through a very difficult time. And I'm not sure I would have made it without her. Well, you know how she was round here most days. Helping out with the cooking and the cleaning. Popping over to see if we were OK, if we needed anything . . . I thought . . . Well . . . Shit, Christopher, I'm trying to keep this simple . . . I thought she might carry on coming over. I thought . . . and maybe I was being stupid . . . I thought she might . . . eventually . . . want to move in here. Or that we might move into her house. We . . . we got on really, really well. I thought we were friends. And I guess I thought wrong. I guess . . . in the end . . . it comes down to . . . Shit . . . We argued, Christopher, and . . . She said some things I'm not going to say to you because they're not nice, but they hurt, but . . . I think she cared more for that bloody dog than for me, for us. And maybe that's not so stupid, looking back. Maybe we are a bloody handful. And maybe it is easier living on your own looking after some stupid mutt than sharing your life with other actually human beings. I mean, shit, buddy, we're not exactly low-maintenance, are we . . . ?

Curse of the Starving Class
Sam Shepard

Play
35+
Seriocomic

Weston, the drunken head of an abysmally dysfunctional family, comes home after a bender to an empty refrigerator.

(*Loud sound of garbage cans being knocked over. WESTON enters.*) WHO PUT THE GODDAMN GARBAGE CANS RIGHT IN FRONT OF THE GODDAMN DOOR?

(*Crosses to the refrigerator and opens it.*) Perfect! ZERO! ABSOLUTELY ZERO! NADA! GOOSE EGGS! (*He yells at the house in general.*) WE'VE DONE IT AGAIN! WE'VE GONE AND LEFT EVERYTHING UP TO THE OLD MAN AGAIN! ALL THE UPKEEP! THE MAINTENANCE! PERFECT!

(*Slams the refrigerator door.*) I don't even know why we keep a refrigerator in this house. All it's good for is slamming. Slams all day long and through the night. SLAM! SLAM! SLAM! What's everybody hoping for, a miracle! IS EVERY-BODY HOPING FOR A MIRACLE?

THERE'S NO MORE MIRACLES! NO MIRACLES TODAY! THEY'VE BEEN ALL USED UP! IT'S ONLY ME! MR. SLAVE LABOR HIMSELF COME HOME TO REPLEN-ISH THE EMPTY LARDER!

Curse of the Starving Class

Sam Shepard

Play
40+
Seriocomic

Weston, the drunken head of an abysmally dysfunctional family, learns his wife is trying to sell the house and property with the assistance of sleazy con artist.

I'll find him. Then I'll find that punk who sold me that phony desert land. I'll track them all down. Every last one of them. Your mother too. I'll track her down and shoot them in their bed. In their hotel bed. I'll splatter their brains all over the vibrating bed. I'll drag him into the hotel lobby and slit his throat. I was in the war. I know how to kill. I was over there. I know how to do it. I've done it before. It's not a big deal. You just make an adjustment. You convince yourself it's all right. That's all. It's easy. You just slaughter them. Easy.

He doesn't know what he's dealing with. He thinks I'm just like him. Cowardly. Sniveling. Sneaking around. He's not counting on what's in my blood. He doesn't realize the explosiveness. We don't belong to the same class. He doesn't realize that. He's not counting on that. He's counting on me to use my reason. To talk things out. To have a conversation. To go out and have a business lunch and talk things over. He's not counting on murder. Murder's the farthest thing from his mind.

Curse of the Starving Class
Sam Shepard

Play
40+
Dramatic

Weston, a newly reformed alcoholic and head of an abysmally dysfunctional family, watches his son Wesley gorge himself before the refrigerator in animalistic protest of his emotional starvation.

Look, I know I ignored some a' the chores around the place and you had to do it instead a' me. But I brought you some artichokes back, didn't I? Didn't I do that? I didn't have to do that. I went outa' my way. Saw the sign on the highway and drove two miles outa' my way just to bring you back some artichokes. (*Nervously watches WESLEY eating.*)

You couldn't be all that starving! We're not that bad off, goddamnit! I've seen starving people in my time, and we're not that bad off! (*No reaction from WESLEY, who continues to eat ravenously.*)

You just been spoiled, that's all! This is a paradise for a young person! There's kids your age who'd give their eyeteeth to have an environment like this to grow up in! You've got everything! Everything! Opportunity is glaring you in the teeth here! (. . .)

If this is supposed to make me feel guilty, it's not working! It's not working because I don't have to pay for my past now! Not after this morning! All that's behind me now! YOU UNDERSTAND ME? IT'S ALL OVER WITH BECAUSE I'VE BEEN REBORN! I'M A WHOLE NEW PERSON NOW! I'm a whole new person.

Cuthbert's Last Stand

Andrew Biss

Play
Early 20s
Dramatic

Cuthbert's mother has raised Cuthbert since early childhood in the hope and belief that he is homosexual. She has just been mocking her son in front of the young male guest that she has brought home as a possible suitor.

That's right, go ahead and laugh. Laugh away. Get it *all* out of your system. Because when I've finished what I'm about to say, I doubt very much that laughter is going to be among your top ten list of immediate responses. (*With great difficulty.*) You see, I . . . I've no idea how many times I've attempted to tell you this in the past . . . and how many times my courage has simply up and left me, but I . . . I can't maintain this façade any longer, Mother. I can't continue with the lies . . . the deceit . . . the pretense. I can't go on saying one thing and feeling another. You see, the fact is, Mother, as hard as this is going to be for you to accept . . . or understand—especially when sober—the fact remains . . . the fact remains I am not the person you think I am. The painful truth is . . . (*Taking a deep breath.*) I am not . . . and as far as I know, never have been . . . a homosexual. (*Beat.*) Well? Aren't you going to say something? Aren't you going to tell me how . . . disappointed you are? How I've let you down? How ashamed you feel? (*Beat.*) I know this has to be difficult to take in, but I . . . I had to tell you. I couldn't continue living this make-believe existence any longer. (*Beat, then pensively.*) And now that I have told you, I . . . Well, I feel

. . . I feel wonderful, actually. And yet at the same time quite dreadful. Dreadful because . . . because I feel as though I've just taken the entire image of everything that you thought I was and smashed it into little tiny pieces.

Daddy Garbage

John Edgar Wideman

Short Story
30+
Dramatic

Strayhorn tells John French of a shocking discovery.

French, I found a dead baby this morning. (. . .) Shhh. Don't
be shouting. This ain't no McKinley's nor nobody else's business. Listen to what I'm telling you and don't make no fuss.
Found a baby. All wrapped up in newspaper and froze stiff as a
board. Somebody put it in a box and threw the box in the trash
back of Dumferline. (. . .) It's the God-awful truth. Daddy
Garbage on our way this morning up the alley. The dog, he
found it. Turned over a can, the box fell out. I almost kicked it,
John French. Almost kicked the pitiful thing. (. . .) Laid in the
garbage like wasn't nothing but spoilt meat. (. . .) Just a little
bitty thing. Wasn't no need to look hard to know it was dead.

Daddy's Home
Henry W. Kimmel

Play
40+
Seriocomic

A stay-at-home dad, Syd Devine, has a moment of truth. He carries a baseball mitt.

I'm glad I devoted myself to the kids—although I wonder if I was truly with them—or whether I was really just there to take them from one activity to another—which was fine for them—but, still, I wonder how much of it passed me by—while it was sitting right in front of them. A sunny Tuesday afternoon—where did it go? On paper, I did a lot for my son: I was his room parent eight years in a row. I—at least my wife did—made sure he could play the piano by the time he was eight. I had him playing organized baseball, soccer and tennis—sometimes in the same day. And yet, was I any different to him than my dad was to me? I wonder if on my deathbed I'm going to say, I wish I spent more time at the office.

Dangerous Dave
and the Whalers

Lawrence Krauser

Original Monologue
20s-30s
Comic

*Jim Butterfly, an actor, responds to the question: "Have you
ever played Hamlet?"*

Have I? Or have not I?
That's a very good question . . .
(Should I stay faithful to memory's song
which stings and harrows my ear with bit parts,
or with charms dissemble and deny my regrets,
and by falsehood reverse them? To remember,
to gloat; and by a lie to say I played
the role a thousand times on a thousand stages—
'Tis a role an actor should have played.
But to play, to perform, perchance before a crowd
including critics—and in print receive a snub—
that's a curtain from which no career is called.
A writ pan of your shot at the supreme role
encountered in a scrapbook years later, reminiscing—
Ouch! There's the curse of the printed word;
for who would study the shape and sound of letters;
memorize the part; don Danish costumery;
suffer direction, the envy of uncast princes,
the insolence of understudies, the afterglare
of classic renditions by box-office titans,
only to have his fond nostalgia unmade
by a pedant's ancient sneer? Yikes! Never!)
—Of *course* I played Hamlet!

Dear Chuck

Jonathan Dorf

Play
Teen
Dramatic

A swim club. The actor perhaps holds a rubber ducky, a towel, and whatever else would make him suitably dressed to go swimming. The actor points at a lifeguard.

I should totally get a lawyer and sue that guy. (. . .) Don't give me that look like you don't know what I'm talkin' about. Playin' dumb isn't gonna' keep me out of the kiddie pool. The sign doesn't even say "kiddie pool." It says "wading pool." I want to wade. I'm real big on wading. I wade at the beach. I wade in the pond near my house, even waded in the Dead Sea once, which is really hard 'cause all the salt makes you float. Who am I bothering if I wade here? I mean hey—I'm probably the only person in there that wouldn't change the color of the water.

(Pause.)

The lifeguard says maybe if there's nobody else in the pool he'd let me swim. So I'm watchin'. The kids from the summer camp are at the snack bar having their afternoon cookies and bug juice, so they're all getting out. But just as the camp kids are finally gone, there's this one little twerp—looks like he's two, maybe three—got those elbow flotation things, and he's crying his head off and his mom or nanny or housekeeper or whatever is draggin' him in. He obviously doesn't want to go—he's trying to bite her hand—so why doesn't this crazy lady just give the kid some time to get over it and stop scarring him for life. Because I don't want to see him turn into a psychopathic killer, and I don't own a bathtub, so this way, everybody gets what they want.

(Pause.) (. . .)

I'm thinkin' about a petition. Or a boycott. Or maybe a march where everybody sings "We Shall Overcome." A lot. In a round. Because this is age discrimination, and it really sucks.

The Death of King Arthur
Matthew Freeman

Play
Teens
Dramatic

The young page, in the midst of Camelot's unraveling, presents an idealistic and hopeful view of heroism.

Today my blade lays lonesome siege to the stronghold of a Beast. My wooden rapier is alone today, but does a valiant hero need more than strength and purity? Ah no! By Arthur, I have learned that courage makes a Knight, and Might comes after Right. One day I will be with him. When I am taller, I'll travel to the Land of Gore, to save the Maid Melinda from the wiry bloodroots and Black Sorcerer. My wooden rapier made sharper with use, you see, so I can wield it skillful. The sweet Melinda will be married to me before the King. But not before I've faced above a pit of fire, her captor and outwitted him with riddles. He'd say: "Stand down, small knight! Your age impedes your might!" And I, with Maiden's hand in mine, quip: "Mother said as much this morning . . . long before I felled the wiry roots! But you know as much as Mother, villain, there's none too young for bravery!" And by Excalibur, he'd pause for a retort, and in his leg! Then ARM! Then . . . other ARM! Can you see me then? I'm not noble, I know. But Arthur was raised by farmers. I'll see him and he'll see me in him. I'll teach the King a move or two with my cutter! I will be the Child of the Round Table.

The Death of King Arthur
Matthew Freeman

Play
Teens
Dramatic

Mordred, King Arthur's illegitimate son of incest, finalizes his plans to expose Lancelot and Guenevere.

Evolution of the English honor.
We'll tempt the Good King to discover Lust.
In that action we'll serve your righteous lies
Turned truth by luck, and with your Christ
We'll turn his Holy Grail to memorial.
Go off, and prepare arguments and twists.
I'll meet thee in due time before the King.
(Exit Agravaine.)
Before the King? Before my father-uncle
I'll report and turn the prevailing tides
As tide and moon together seem to meet
Conspire and plan their constant connection.
So I, the moonchild, pull the waves of fire
Upon my devil daddy Arthur of the Water.
If there is anything true about father
It is he is a myth. He's smoke and mirrors
Raised unregal farmer and placed to rule
On warrior throne by succubus son.
By British fools he's praised as Christian King,
Though sons abound, his married life newfound.
But this strange religion is lost on one
Who is a King's unrighteous incest seed

And born of prophecy to crush and lead.
When before Arthur his friends kneel in shame
And Guenevere is shown as skin and bones
We'll see who England loves as ruler loved
And who she shuns as all too far away.
Good night, old Knight, is all that they shall say.

Dinner with Friends
Donald Margulies

Play
40s
Dramatic

Two couples—Karen and Gabe, Tom and Beth—are old friends. Tom has left Beth for another woman. Here, Gabe explains to Tom what he has done.

So when you repudiate your entire adult life . . . (. . .)

That's *essentially* what you've done. And I can understand how you might find it necessary to do that: It must be strangely exhilarating blowing everything to bits. (. . .)

I mean it. You build something that's precarious in even the best of circumstances and you succeed, or at least you make it *look* like you've succeeded, your *friends* think you have, you had *us* fooled, and then, one day, you blow it all up! It's like, I watch Danny and Isaac sometimes, dump all their toys on the floor, Legos and blocks and train tracks, and build these elaborate cities together. They'll spend hours at it, they'll plan and collaborate, and squabble and negotiate, but they'll do it. And then what do they do? They wreck it! No pause to revel in what they accomplished, no sigh of satisfaction, they just launch into a full-throttle attack, bombs bursting, and tear the whole damn thing apart.

Dog Chameleon
Eric Bogosian

Play
30s+
Seriocomic

Eric rails against the high cost of normalcy.

Hey, I want to be normal, just like every other guy! (. . .) I want to yell at my wife when she goes on a spending spree! I want to help my kids with the grades! I want to fertilize my lawn. I want to order my hamburger *my way*! I want to donate money to impoverished minorities!

But all that stuff costs money. Being normal is expensive, you know? (. . .)

I want to be rich. And I want to be famous. These are normal desires that should not be thwarted. If you thwart them, if you repress them, you get cancer.

Shit, I want *fame*! Look at *me*, man! Fame is what counts. Fame with money. Any jerk can go to the top of some tower with a scope rifle and start shooting at people. That's shitty fame. I want the good kind. The kind with lots and lots of money. Any slob can win the lottery, it takes *skill* and *brains* to get the fame and the money *at the same time* . . . that's success, man. So everyone looks at you, wherever you go, and they say, "That guy, he did it. He got everybody to look at him, admire him and give him money, their money, at the same time!"

I heard about this guy, he made four-hundred-million dollars. Four-hundred-million dollars! I'd be happy with fifty million.

Down the Road

Lee Blessing

Play
Late 20s
Dramatic

In response to the question "What was it like with your first victim?" serial killer William Reach gives the interviewer exactly what he asks for.

You want to know how it feels? I'll tell you. It feels like . . . the middle of space. Floating. Alone. Driving late at night on a deserted road. Headed directly into a perfect dark that somehow gets darker. And the road and woods and sky all roll up together into a huge gateway that's always opening—just opening as you get there. The feeling of the steering wheel and the dashboard is so familiar, so . . . owned by you. The girl—the victim—is in the seat beside you. And you're more alone than if she wasn't there. You understand? *(A beat.)* A lot of guys would try to deny this. But I feel we can be honest here, don't you? *(A beat.)* That victim owes you her breath. It's not hers anymore—from the time she trusted you. From the time she failed to protect herself. If you don't want her to breathe, if it gets to you, at any point—what do you do? Dan?

[Dan: You kill her.]

East Texas Hot Links

Eugene Lee

Play
58
Dramatic

Adolph, a blind old sage and disabled veteran, spends most of his time and money in the Top o' the Hill Café, East Texas, 1955.

You ain't never been hungry. When I was in the war you had men tryin' to kill one 'nother over a damn grasshopper. Hungry! Hungry enough to need to see something die. That damn starvation is a son'ne gun. Starvation of the stomach . . . the soul . . . the spirit. When starvation starts to set in . . . sense steps aside. You stop thinkin' 'cause all you can do is feel. Since that shit blew up in my face . . . my eyes been on a diet of darkness. Truth be told tho' . . . I see better in the dark. Ain't even got to close my eyes to dream. (. . .) Yeah, I got leftovers in my head. I remember what this place used to look like when Baby David ran it. I 'member what most of you looked like back then. I 'member what I looked like. I remember 'bout every book I ever read, too. That's why I wallow in what I've seen and learned. 'Cause it's all I get.

East Texas Hot Links
Eugene Lee

Play
35
Dramatic

*Roy, former high school basketball star, relives his glory days in
front of his friends at Charlesetta's Top o' the Hill Café, East
Texas, 1955.*

It's in the record book. You can look it up. I damn near single-
handedly out-scored damn near every team they could convince
to get on the court with me. Shit! Averaged thirty-three points a
game! Reboundin'! Coach said to me just the other day. I seen
him, on his to way fishin' . . . He said he ain't never coached a
better player. Now that's from the coach. (. . .)

We was the best in the state of Texas. (. . .) The best colored schools from Dallas to Lubbock walked off the court
shakin' they heads and cryin' and shit. If they'da played us
'gainst the whites it woulda been embarrassin' to 'em. We had
some boys . . . James Smith and them long-arm'd Colter
boys . . . who could run and jump and put that ball in that
hole like myself. I used to love, to hear them drawers pop.
WHHPT! People in the bleachers would be fallin' out. Women
screamin' my name. Roy Moore! Charlesetta know. We was
beatin' teams by twenty ta thirty points. (. . .)

I got the keys to the gym and I'll whup your ass 'til it rope
like okra. I plays me some basketball still. It be hard to top that
in my life. Unless Charlesetta come on 'round and admit she in
love with me.

East Texas Hot Links

Eugene Lee

Play
33
Dramatic

Community members, gathered in Charlesetta's Top o' the Hill Café (East Texas, 1955) are growing uneasy with XL's chumminess with his white boss. Here, XL further alienates himself as he defines his view of the world.

Ain't nary one of the rest of you offered to buy me nothin'. Just 'cause I'mo buy 'Lumbus a beer don't mean I want to spend all my money helpin' the rest of y'all get drunk. That's what's wrong with the average colored man now. Take kindness for weakness. I don't want to be read wrong by nobody. That's just the way I am. I don't know no other way to be. I ain't sayin' I won't help somebody . . . if I can. I don't mix business and pleasure. If I'mo help you . . . we can make us a deal . . . in like a business kinda situation. Shit, beyond that I ain't got no kids, no wife, everybody in my family got families of they own. I ain't responsible for nobody but mine own self. Been like that since I was thirteen. Talkin' 'bout chains. I ain't got nothin' to do with no kind of chains.

Eating Round the Bruise

Barret O'Brien

Play
20s-30s
Seriocomic

A high school civics teacher has a minor meltdown in front of the class.

It's a bumper sticker revolution, kids. Thousands of years of history boiled down to . . . what? *(Measures with his hands.)* Eight by three? Ten by . . . My Karma ran over my Dogma. My Karma ran over my Dogma. That's funny. *(Singles out a member of the class.)* Craig, What does the bumper sticker on your car say? Jesus Saves. Save Our Lake. Proud NRA Member. Well it's got to be something. Choose your message, son. Times ticking. Miles are being burned without a slogan. What will the good people behind you do at traffic lights? Give them something to read, boy. No? So you're content to snicker and pass notes in my class. Fair enough. You're young. What are you . . . seventeen? No? Eighteen? I see. You vote? A shrug. That a yes or a no? You don't know. Do you remember pushing a button or filling in a Scantron sheet anytime yesterday? No? Then you didn't vote. Get out of my class. Get up and get out. Anyone want to join him? Put down your hands. This morning you all became citizens of a new country—an intolerant, fearful, violent, ignorant country . . . and you . . . Where are your picket signs? Picket signs, where are your rifles? Why are you standing for this? Which of you is my revolutionary? Anyone? Dawn? Jude, you the one with explosives in your locker? Are you the one going to make me heard? Burn yourself on the White House lawn? Do something. For me. Anything. Now. Might be . . . enough.

Eclipse
Andrea Lepcio

Play
20+
Comic

Al, trying desperately to understand, stumbles his way through a come-on.

But, of course, you're saying . . . you've, kind of, been with men too. *(She indicates no.)* So you are a virgin—not that I fully understand the mechanics of lesbianism—but presumably you are still, technically. I'm just trying to understand . . . I mean, you must have . . . it's hard to believe, OK, you wouldn't at least . . . how it even occurred to you . . . let alone . . . There's two things I'm trying to ask here . . . correct me if I'm wrong . . . but I, kind of, thought women turned to women when things didn't, like, work out with men . . . not that you're the type of woman that couldn't work things out, OK, on the contrary. And secondly, how . . . when did you, kind of, have the . . . like, nerve to . . . or was it some older gym teacher? I just can't imagine you looking at girls the way I do . . . I mean, cheerleaders, Playboy bunnies for cripessake . . . The bottom line, OK, is how . . . without even, OK, trying . . . you must have wanted at some point, I mean, at least a little human curiosity. Opposites do attract. The Penis.

Eloise & Ray

Stephanie Fleischmann

Play
28
Dramatic

Ray, speaking in poetic stream-of-consciousness, tells of falling for Eloise, his arch-enemy's sister.

I am one of the BOYS of the boys of the boys of the one of the Blood-brother-dynamic-duo-action-packed-/ /in-cahoots-smooth-moving-partners-in-crime-Boys. One of the— The two of us. Him. And me. Like sand and water.

(. . .) Seven years. Sandpaper pain scraping upside my head. Seven years. Adding up and taking over. So that all of a sudden it was time. To get even. To freeze him up. Wherever his legs had run their course. To throw a blow back in the direction of HIS stomach— When there she was. His. Even. Little sister twister shadow. So even. And me— I am— I was— One of the— She— is— She is a girl. Some strange kind of girl woman girl. All she gotta to do is look in my direction and the scraping pain IS gone.

So I got even. I did what I had to do, only I didn't expect— I mean— How was I to know what I would feel? Too much girl-woman-girl for— For me. So I ditched her. What else could I do? I came back here. Me and Jed. Small town boys. Jewelry store hours from home. Nothing better to do than kick up some trouble. Here in Trouble, Texas, Scene of the Crime. Only— I been away from her one day and it's here. Sandpaper pain upside my head— Oh it's getting worse. It's bad.

What I need is water. My cure-all. Eloise. Me and her. Like sand and water.

Eloise & Ray

Stephanie Fleischmann

Play
28
Dramatic

Ray is in love with Eloise. He imagines her next to him.

What I like about Eloise is her size. She's a little bitty thing of a girl. Compact, so you can fold her up. Put her in a box and keep her. Fold her, hold her in your arms. That she is small means she is more easily mine. (. . .) I can lift her high up in the air. (. . .) Hold her upside down and shake her. If she needs to be taught. Like the time I give her the pearl.

(. . .) She swallows the pearl. So I don't got no choice. 'Cept to hold her, fold her. Upside down. And shake her. It's what she needs. I give her that pearl, see, because a pearl is sand and water. I am the sand and Eloise is the water. We got both of the two right here. Both of the two. *(He stops shaking. Stares at her face hanging upside down.)*

Ocean a million miles away. *(Starts shaking again.)*

That she is small means I can lift her high up in the air. Shake her long and hard, until the pearl comes spitting out. A pellet of a pearl. A Pez. My Eloise a Pez dispenser out of order, Pez pellets round and hard and sharp as BB's made of steel coming flying out of her mouth. Little and small as she is, my BB gun of a girl. So I shake her and shake her and the pearl comes flying out and she is crying and that's when I hold her close, never once letting her feet touch the ground. Hold her, fold her there for a while. Because that's what she needs. She needs to be taught.

Everybody Knew Bubba Riff
John Edgar Wideman

Short Story
Teen-20s
Dramatic

The narrator riffs about an abusive father figure.

[S]it back on down where you was sitting drinking your wine before you got all up in my face about nothing cause you ain't my real daddy and you can wave your finger and holler all you want but if you ever lay a hand on me again I'ma break you in half old man don't care how much my mama need the shit you bring around here no more whipping on me you touch me or put a hand on her ever again it's rumble time mano a mano motherfucker me and you on the green and if you can't stand the heat get out the kitchen this ain't no Papa Bear Mama Bear and li'l Sugar Baby Bear jam no more I'm grown now ain't taking your whiskeyhead shit no more hit my mama hit me I'ma bust you up (. . .)

Falcons

D. Travers Scott

Original Monologue
12
Dramatic

*Kurt is the twelve-year-old son of a mentally ill single father,
who is often unemployed. During the day Kurt and his seven-
year-old brother, Kris, beg for spare change in the city parks of
Seattle, and at night he tells his father stories of their day.*

I told Dad about the falcons after he come get us, how I
learned 'bout them from this drunk in the park. I usually stay
away from drunks 'cause they might fuck with me and Kris,
but we were making good change down by his corner. So this
old drunk, he pointed up at this building and showed me
specks to watch for. He said if'n you went up on top that building, you'd find lots of bloody, dead pigeons the falcons eat. Dad
said royal ladies and knights back in King Arthur times used to
train falcons to hunt; they'd fly off and kill, then come back
and land on your hand. I told Dad, when you see the falcons as
a bigger speck, and they do this funny curl and meet a tiny
spot, that means they're teaching their kids to hunt. The falcons
kill a pigeon and carry it in their claws. They fly out and flip
over upside-down, holding the pigeon up for the little falcon.
The little one swoops down and tries to take it from its parent's
claws. Dad had never heard of that. He thought the drunk was
just trying to get me to look up so's he could swipe our change.

Feast of Love
Charles Baxter

Novel
40s
Comic

Bradley Smith is manager of Jitters, a coffee shop in a mall, and has been married twice.

You know what I hate? I hate it when someone turns to me and says, "What're you thinking, Bradley? Tell me. What're you *thinking*?" Well, no. If it's a-penny-for-your-thought time, here's your penny back. Because, first of all, it's private, whatever my thoughts are—and don't think I'll tell *you* all my thoughts, either—but secondly, most of the time I don't, in the way of things, *have* any thoughts. There aren't any *thoughts*, per se, is what I'm saying. Day after day it's a long hallway up there, just a yard sale, interrupted with random images of my paintings, or my dog, or the coffee store, or memories, or a woman, her face or her body or something she said, all of it in free fall through the synapses.

And I don't care if I'm mixing my metaphors. This is my second marriage I'm talking about now. I can damn well mix my metaphors on that marriage if I want to. I've got my rights.

Firebug
Todd Ristau

Original Monologue
20+
Dramatic

Author's note: "in a high nasal voice, real fast, dressed like a homeless guy."

Boy, yer tellin' me! I was there the night of the big fire. I was there. I saw the whole thing, man. I saw the people screamin' and jumpin' and the ladies throwin' their babies out the windows so they might has a chance, no chance in the building, man, no fuckin' chance in the building. I remember this one old man, standin' there and lookin' out his third-story window. Real calm and not movin' a muscle while all around him is orange and red fire and like people screamin', brick collapsin' 'cause they ain't got no wooden beams to hold them up no more and this one old man is just standin' there like he ain't afraid of nothin'. He's crazy, somebody says, then some other guy says he might be blind and he don't know what's going on around him. Then I heard that this was a case of him bein' a widow man and he just got nothin' in this life left to lose. (. . .) I go to all the fires. I got one of them scanner things in my van. I like the way people are at fires, so honest and real. Them people in the building, they're real honest. People watchin' are honest too. Honest about being scared, or honest about being worried about the people inside, or just honest about liking to watch stuff burn. Firemen are honest. Cops are honest too. Sometimes I think I might be the only dishonest one at them fires. Well, we'll just have to wait and see what I say if somebody asks me how them fires get started.

Fish Head Soup
Philip Kan Gotanda

Play
30
Dramatic

Mat faked his own death in order to escape his family. Now he has returned to seek money for a film project, but his father has spiraled relentlessly downward, mentally and physically since his son's "funeral." When Mat's film project goes belly up, he wheels his invalid father to the water's edge.

Remember that time downtown? Are you listening to me? Are you listening? Remember that time downtown when that big guy came up to you? "Hey, you a China-man?" You mumbled something and pushed Victor and me into the back seat of the car. (. . .) Victor and I had our noses pressed against the window waiting for you to yell at this ugly man. (. . .) "What, you one of those people from Ja-pan? You a Jap?" He was laughing and having a good time, a crowd had gathered. You finally got in the car but the man was lying on the hood now. I kept thinking, "Why isn't Papa yelling like he does at home (. . .)?"

Are you listening to me?

All the way home, no one said anything. (. . .) And I began to hate you. Hate you because you were my daddy and every time I looked at you I saw you being humiliated, shuffling like a houseboy in front of that man. And you made me feel that same feeling. (. . .)

And so one night I left. Nah, one night I killed myself. Yes, I just killed myself off.

But Papa? I'm back. And you gotta help me this time. This time you gotta help me, you can't leave me in the back seat. Papa? You owe (*Grabbing PAPA by shirt.*) me. You *owe* me. YOU OWE ME!

Five Flights
Adam Bock

Play
32
Comic

Tom is an intense, ballet-loving hockey player.

Of course. Oh yeah of course. I'll go and see it a couple of times. I love the ballet. I'm a hockey player you know so I love it, it's the same in a way, the movement, it's the same, I mean you take Russian nineteenth-century ballet, it's just like a hockey game, it's got five acts, Russian ballet—five acts, act one, narrative it's the story told from beginning to end, act two's a vision, act three is mad scenes, act four the conclusion, act five, a little dance. Now hockey—the game is like the first act of the ballet when the story is told, it's the narrative, the hockey game itself. Then the second act, that's the moment of when it's over, in your mind's eye there's that moment, that critical goal, that incredible, amazing save, or the penalty, that something that was the defining moment that brought us here, it's like act two in the ballet, that moment is a vision. Act three, we won euphoria, or act three, we lost despair, madness, act four, the interviews, the commentary, the coaches' recap, it's all over it's all wrapped up this is what happened this and this and then act five I have to go dance because I'm so fired up I couldn't go to bed. I gotta go dance. I gotta keep moving. I love the ballet.

Five Scenes from Life
Alan Brody

Play
20s-30s
Dramatic

Bobby, an inmate at a federal prison, speaks to the volunteer Government teacher, Nina. A guard stands just outside the classroom.

Listen. (. . .) I *like* you. That's all I'm trying to say. I'm not talking about dirty pictures. I'm not talking about goons like Mendes who got their hands in their pockets all the time. I'm talking *like*. (. . .)

Just let me tell you. We've had lady teachers before. And I've sat there with all the other goons watching movies in my head while she talked about the English Romantics or supply and demand and thought she was doing just fine in the field. I came in here all ready to use you like that, too. But you arrive dressed, you know, just right with that blouse buttoned so your neck was open and the collar fell so that was all. Not scared, not pushing. Just right. And you got down to business. We could tell you knew what we were thinking, and you just let us. And yeah, I was thinking it, too, but it kept turning into something else. Every time you smiled when some other lady teacher would have laughed too hard, or when you listened to one of us and came back—bam—dead on the target so it showed you were really listening, I could feel it turn into something else. I thought, hey, I like this lady. I'd like to *talk* to her. So I just wanted you to know. You make me feel warm without burning, y'understand me? That's all I meant. And I wanted to tell you.

Fool Circle
S. W. Senek

Play
25-30
Comic

Lawrence is in a coffee shop, looking for a date and a place to sit. He glances at Delores, then sits at the table next to her.

Look, I don't mean to bother you, but if we should ever date I want you to know I hate ramblers. I've had too many dates that talk on and on about nothing. But not me. That's one thing you'll notice right away. I don't ramble. I can control myself. I'm in complete control of this here vehicle. Oh, yes. From point A to point B. Speaking of point A to B—I couldn't help noticing how cold it was when I was walking here? *Unquestionably* cold. *(Beat.)* Did you ever go about your day— stop in the middle of your lunch hour, while eating pastrami on rye, and say to yourself, "Duh, I wore the wrong shoes." I have four pairs of shoes: Two pairs of sneakers; then a brand-spanking-new brown dress shoe, and lastly, the "New York" black casual shoe—perfect for any occasion. The only problem with my black casual is there's a massive hole on the left heel. I can't toss it—there's been too much emotion invested. Besides, when I put it on this morning, the weatherman said the forecast was "bone dry." Bone dry? Where did they get that saying, "bone dry." Before you know it, slush soaks up in my black dress sock—and I spend the rest of my outdoor afternoon experiences limping. Between the limping and the holiday bell ringers ringing in your ear—The point is, for the next twenty minutes you still have this reverberation in your head. I like holidays but there's just too many. Maybe we could reduce it by one or combine all of them—you know, take Hanukkah, Kwanza, Christmas—make it one sizeable holiday. We could say, "Happy Hana-Kwanz-Mas" *(Sings)* "Have yourself a merry Hana-Kwanz-Mas." . . . "I'm dreaming of a white Hana-Kwanz-Mas." *(Beat.)* I'm rambling, right?

Freefall
Charles Smith

Play
20s
Dramatic

Spoon is a streetwise Chicago drug dealer who "would be working for IBM if born of another race or class." He tries to convince his friend Monk, recently released from prison, to join him.

You see, I am what's known as financially stable. I have money in the bank and I have the best type job security there is. I will never be laid off, the company I work for will never close down, tough economic times is something I hear about only on the radio. And do you know why? Because of supply and demand, my brother, the theory upon which this country was built. Now I don't know about your friend Mr. Rickey, but I see you standing here going through the garbage collecting the shit that other people threw away. So, after you wear out your first pair of shoes from crushing cans and walking to the redemption center, you come see me, Monk. You're smart. You got a good level head on your shoulders. And now that you are a college graduate as well as a member of the Brotherhood, I am obligated to get you up and operating. Smile, my brother. Ain't nothing out there but a bunch of fatted calves and we gonna take them all off. One by one.

Freefall
Charles Smith

Play
20s-30s
Dramatic

Monk, recently out of prison, challenges his middle-class sister-in-law, Alex.

Oh no, my lady, I may be many things, but an animal I am not. If anything, I am more like a trapeze artist, up there on that trapeze, a thousand feet in the air swinging back and forth just like the mutherfucker at the circus you saw. Only difference is, there is no net below me. There's nothing below me but rock solid concrete. So when it comes time for me to make a move, when I have to let go of that bar and reach out, I have got to make sure that there is a hand out there somewhere to catch me, cause if not, I go into a freefall. A freefall without a net, from a thousand feet in the air with nothing but stone cold concrete below. So don't talk to me about throwing my life away. You, who got her nets spread out all over the fuckin' place. You can do all the double twists and back flips you want 'cause no matter what happens, you got somebody there to catch you. (. . .) So don't talk to me about throwing my life away. All I'm doing is making sure that somewhere out there is a hand, one hand that will catch me if I fall.

Freefall
Charles Smith

Play
30s+
Dramatic

Grant, a middle-class, tightly wound Chicago desk cop, confronts his wife about their holiday plans.

I can't do it, Alex. Every year for Christmas we visit your family. And every year you're surrounded by the faces and places you're familiar with Every year you go into your room and show me all of your tennis trophies and the plaque you won when you were on the debate team. Every year you pull out all your old stuffed animals and line them up on the bed, and every year it all looks so foreign to me. Well, this year I want to spend Christmas in my own home. I want to be around the things that are familiar to me. This year, I don't want to live anybody else's memories. This year, I need to take time and look over my own.

Fur and Other Dangers
Allyson Currin

Play
30s
Seriocomic

Boots is the alpha cat from hell.

She's calling me.
I'm not responding.
I'm torturing her.
They think I haven't noticed.
They think I'm so naïve. Like I don't understand about the birds and the bees.
Like I didn't grow up in the alley.
Like I wouldn't get it when her belly started to swell up like Muffy's did that time she delivered eight.
Well, I do.
And I'm pissed.
I hope they don't expect me to make any sacrifices for this.
This chair is mine.
That little spot in front of the refrigerator is mine, too. And I don't intend to move just because they need to get to the baby formula at four o'clock in the morning.
Don't get that idea.
Filling my water dish should still be their priority whenever they're in the bathroom.
And if they think for one moment that whatever red-faced demon seed they've spawned is kicking me out of the master bed at night, then it will make me more than happy to pee all over their imported eiderdown coverlet. That'll teach 'em.

No litter of hers will ever usurp my control over this house. Not when I have worked so tirelessly for so many years to make it run according to exact specifications and desires. Power mad, you say? Ah, perhaps.
(*Beat*). Like I care. (*Hisses loudly.*)

The Girl on the
Red Velvet Swing
Tim Monsion

Film script
30
Dramatic

New York, 1903. Thaw warns Miss Evelyn Nesbit about get-
ting involved with Stanford White, the famous architect. Thaw
later murders White, in front of Evelyn, at White's rooftop
theater at Madison Square Garden.

Why? Because he's a beast, Miss Nesbit. You have no future
with him. He brings young women to ruin. There have been
many others, you know; don't think you're the first. Have you
heard the story of Annie Johnson? No older than you, at one of
those stag dinners he throws. The centerpiece was a large pie, a
real pie, six feet in diameter, and poor Annie was the filling.
The band struck up "Sing a Song of Sixpence" and when the
pie was opened, out popped Annie, a shivering, tender flower,
naked for all to see. Sixteen years old. Two days later, she disappeared. Ashamed. They say she's buried in Potters Field. Oh,
the newspapers don't talk about his parties, because he's from
the upper crust of society.

The Green Man
Todd Ristau

Original Monologue
20+
Dramatic

In every vocation, there is poetry.

They ask me what I do at the hospital. (. . .)

I run the incinerator.

It is my job to sit by the fire,
keep it hot,
and I turn the things that have been cut away,
the damaged and diseased parts of people I don't really know
into carbon.

Carbon is the purest form on earth.

I burn them.
There are no special tools,
I use my hands.
I don't wear gloves or use plastic wrap either . . .
I believe that even a severed limb remains somehow human
and somehow worthy of love and affection.

I couldn't rest if flesh weren't the last thing to touch flesh
before the flames.
One touch before the fire. (. . .)

This morning, these arrived. *(Holds up a brown paper bag.)*

The dancer cried and cried over losing them,
but I think I was the only one
who heard her feet crying over never being useful again . . .

They told me that if I would wait a while to turn them into carbon,
they would teach me to dance.

Ho Ho Hell
Maria Rokas

Play
40s
Comic

*A bitter department-store Santa with a sad past is having a
really bad day.*

Look at them. The greed is suffocating. I'm supposed to be a
saint. Instead I feel like a crack dealer for five-year-olds. Toys,
drugs—what's the difference? Peer pressure, exorbitant costs,
one toy leading to another accessory, and another. It's all
there—a seedy slippery slope they all slide down into my lap.
It's too much. *It's pushing me to the edge.* And all I need is
another nervous kid who's *brilliant* parents bought him a Big
Gulp for lunch only to bypass the bathroom, and stand in the
long line next to the display of miniature tranquility waterfalls,
on the way to *my knee*, where he's going to get all worked up
talking about his favorite toys, and then—oops . . . *(Looking
down at his pant leg.)* They should make these suits out of rubber. What am I saying—suits? *Suit.* The same lousy, worn-out,
filthy rag that waits for me every year like a sad mistress in a
closet in the forgotten recesses of this store *(Putting out his
arms and doing a slow dance with himself.)* for us to do our ritualistic, sad dance together for the dreary month leading up to
Christmas.

Honeymoon
Dane Stauffer

Play
Early 20s
Comic

Jody arrives late for his twin sister's wedding.

I missed the wedding, didn't I? I'm so embarrassed, and I'm
really sorry, and I think this is really a step forward for me, in
that at least I am aware of the fact I am late and I am acknowl-
edging it, even if I am still excusing it defensively and getting
off the issue too quickly, see, I have been learning a lot . . . in
college in my philosophy classes . . . only I would major in
something that has no hope of employment except to teach it to
others, it's like this self-perpetuating thing, it's like lawyers, you
hire 'em to draw up a contract, then you gotta hire 'em to deci-
pher it, but here I am talking when really I'm just . . . sorry . . .
sometimes I think I'm always late because people say you're
always late," and I don't want to disappoint them by not disap-
pointing them, you know, like how sometimes you get tense
trying to avoid tension? But at least Dad videotaped it, like he
videotapes everything, so we can watch it and you know, someday Dad will sit down to watch all the videotapes he's made
and he'll just see videotapes of him . . . videotaping, it's like the
snake eating it's own tail, it's like lawyers and, and philosophy
teachers, it's like holding a mirror up to a mirror and seeing
eternity . . . So, how are you?

Honeymoon in Dealy Plaza

Lawrence Krauser

Play
30+
Comic

A secret agent is torn between duty and his sweet tooth.

She came to me and said look, some fruitcake keeps on sending
me white chocolate, delicious, right, but I don't like white
chocolate, but there's no name on the chocolate, no return
address, how am I gonna get in touch with this person and tell
him thank you very much but please send me dark chocolate—
not milk, she said, she was very specific about this, she pre-
ferred the dark chocolate, the semisweet, and I said, "Mrs.
Onassis," don't you even— Oh I'm sorry, I said "Don't you
even give it a thought, Mrs. *Kennedy*, I'll find out who's sending you the chocolate and don't you ever hesitate to call on me,
ever, I don't care if you go work for the *Russians*, I'm always
here for you." I was just kidding around about that last part,
but here's the thing . . . it's a little embarrassing to admit. But
the thing is, I love white chocolate. She gave me the boxes to
use in my investigation, you know, and—well—I thought I'd eat
just one, for detectivatory purposes. Just one candy, then one
box. But I really do, I mean I *love* white chocolate, and well it
didn't take me very long to eat them all. All the evidence. And I
was too ashamed to . . . We were all so consumed with grief in
those days. That was one hell of a difficult winter.

Horrible Child

Lawrence Krauser

Play
Pre-teen
Dramatic

Horrible, a child, is horrible.

An arm's length for you, for me ten thousand yards—
I see there ten cards, I got five. I live
like a maggot off your ill-processed feast;
to my yeast rise your flour, to the west set the hour;
no time. So flow the sources of my remorses.
So what, I'm Horrible, leave me alone.
Go smother your gardens, scratch your horizons
Go grow beneath you brambles of cobras
I'm Horrible and that's what is,
that sums up the dumb nut of your oafish ravings
the depleted savings of your rusted tabernacle;
I'm Horrible and it ain't gonna change.
I'm Horrible as they come and I come harder,
I'm Horrible as I come and as they goes,
I'm Horrible as I come and as I doze,
Horrible—*c'est moi*; Horrible—*autre fois*;
I'm Horrible as It gets 'cause I am It;
Why don't you run?

The Hours
Michael Cunningham

Novel
40s
Dramatic

Richard, mildly delusional as he dies of AIDS, confesses to his oldest friend, Clarissa, his dissatisfaction with his last novel.

Can I tell you an embarrassing secret? Something I've never told anyone? (. . .)

I thought I was a genius. I actually used that word, privately, to myself. (. . .) Oh, pride, pride. I was so wrong. It defeated me. It simply proved insurmountable. There was so much, oh, far too much for me. I mean, there's the weather, there's the water and the land, there are the animals, and the buildings, and the past and the future, there's space, there's history. There's this thread or something caught between my teeth, there's the old woman across the way, did you notice she switched the donkey and the squirrel on her windowsill? And, of course, there's time. And place. And there's you, Mrs. D. I wanted to tell part of the story of part of you. Oh, I'd love to have done that. (. . .) But everything's left out of it, almost everything. And then I just stuck on a shock ending. Oh, now, I'm not looking for sympathy, really. We want so much, don't we? (. . .)

I don't have any regrets, really, except that one. I wanted to write about you, about us, really. Do you know what I mean? I wanted to write about everything, the life we're having and the lives we might have had. I wanted to write about all the ways we might die.

The Hours
Michael Cunningham

Novel
40s
Dramatic

On the night he is to be celebrated, Richard, a suicidal author dying of AIDS, sits precariously on a windowsill. He speaks to his oldest friend, Clarissa.

I took the Xanax *and* the Ritalin. They work wonderfully together. I feel wonderful. I opened all the blinds, but still, I found I wanted more air and light. I had a hard time getting up here, I don't mind telling you. (. . .)

I don't think I can make it to the party. (. . .) I'm sorry. (. . .)

I don't know if I can face this. You know. The party and the ceremony, and then the hour after that, and the hour after that. (. . .) One and another and you get through that one and then, my god, there's another. I'm so sick. (. . .)

I've felt it for some time now, closing around me like the jaws of a gigantic flower. Isn't that a peculiar analogy? It feels that way, though. It has a certain vegetable inevitability. Think of the Venus flytrap. Think of kudzu choking a forest. It's a sort of juicy, green, thriving progress. Toward, well, you know. The green silence. Isn't it funny that, even now, it's difficult to say the word "death"?

How I Learned to Drive
Paula Vogel

Play
45
Dramatic

Uncle Peck, married to Aunt Mary, drops in on Li'l Bit in her dorm room. He has been obsessed with her for years.

Li'l Bit—you're scared. Your mother and your grandparents have filled your head with all kinds of nonsense about men—I hear them working on you all the time—and you're scared. It won't hurt you—if the man you go to bed with really loves you. And I have loved you since the day I held you in my hand. (. . .)

Li'l Bit. Listen. Listen. (. . .) Li'l Bit—I'm going to ask you just this once. Of your own free will. Just lie down on the bed with me—our clothes on—just lie down with me, a man and a woman . . . and let's . . . hold one another. Nothing else. Before you say anything else. I want the chance to . . . hold you. Because sometimes the body knows things that the mind isn't listening to . . . (. . .)

Do you—do you think of me? (. . .)

I'm forty-five. That's not old for a man. And I haven't been able to do anything else but think of you. I can't concentrate on my work—Li'l Bit. You've got to—I want you to think about what I am about to ask you. (. . .)

I want you to be my wife.

Hurlyburly
David Rabe

Play
35+
Comic

While they smoke a joint, Phil explains to Eddie why he's call-
ing it quits with Susie.

You know, I come home in the middle a' the night—she was
out initially with her girlfriends, so naturally I was alone and
went out too. So I come home, I'm ripped, I was on a tear, but
I'm harmless, except I'm on a talking jag, you know, who
cares? She could have some sympathy for the fact that I'm
ripped, she could take that into consideration, let me run my
mouth a little, I'll fall asleep, where's the problem? That's what
you would do for me, right? (. . .)

She can't do that. (. . .)

I'm on a tear, see, I got a theory how to take Las Vegas and
turn it upside down like it's a little rich kid and shake all the
money out of its pockets, right? (. . .)

It was bullshit, Eddie. I was demented and totally ranting,
so to that extent, she was right to pay me no attention, seriously, but she should of faked it.

I Used to Bank Here, But That Was Long, Long Ago

David Rakoff

Short Story
30s+
Dramatic

*David reflects on how cancer altered his connection to the
world.*

Once, on my way home from radiation, a man came running
out of the Knights of Columbus chapter near the hospital.
Another man came running after him and, like a cartoon panel
come to life, the man giving chase actually yelled, "Stop, thief!"
I remember thinking to myself, Well, that's very cliché. I was
close to the robber. I could have stuck my foot out and tripped
him, perhaps. But I didn't. He made it across the street, dodging traffic, and was out of sight in a moment. The man from
the Knights of Columbus stood frustrated on the sidewalk as
the cars rushed by. He turned and gave me a dirty look for my
inaction. I wanted to say something. I wanted to explain how
weak and tired and sick I was at that point. But more than
that, how I had essentially let go of any sense of urgency. I
could lie on a table, they could shoot me full of gamma rays, I
would eat what was put in front of me, the hair could fall from
my head, my throat could be burned. But I was not involved; I
was a stranger here. That he could even see me standing there
seemed vaguely surprising.

Illegal Entry
Clem Martini

Play
17
Dramatic

Garland pleads with fellow delinquent, Stuart, not to set fire to Jim, who lies unconscious before them, to destroy evidence.

Listen. We go back, we take our lumps, we plan, you know, for another day. We go back, *with him*, like he is. And you tell them what happened--and I'll back you up—and it's like, self-defense, you know? Self-defense? They don't put guys in jail for that. (*STUART pours thinner over JIM's body.*)

But you torch him now, *you torch him*, when you didn't have to, and him lying there, and we're really, truly fucked forever. I mean, *I* wouldn't even be able to understand that, man, and I can understand what you did to your dad and other people will too. I mean, you were younger then and look at what he was doing to you . . . all your life, right? I can see that. And other people will too.

(*The thinner bottle is empty. STUART tosses it aside and picks up a lighter.*) But this. This. You gotta listen to me, Stuart, cause I'm on your side.

I don't know what you thought when Jim was saying all that shit about us, about me taking advantage, or whatever, and maybe sometimes, I'm not thinking things through, you know, from your side, 'cause, 'cause—it's hard, getting everything right in your mind about everything, but this is straight,

straight, thinking of you. No bullshit. They'll put us away big time, Stuart. Both of us. They will.

Come on, man, come on. We didn't, you know, go AWOL and all this shit just to get put in the pen, right? It's enough for tonight, eh? Stuart? It's enough.

I'm Not Rappaport
Herb Gardner

Play
60+
Seriocomic

Midge protects his park bench from Nat, an elderly "intruder."

(Remains seated, slowly circling his fists in the air like a boxer.)

You read them hands? Study them hands, boy. Them hands wore Golden Gloves, summer of Nineteen and Twenty-Four. This here's *my* spot, *been* my spot six months now, my good and peaceful spot till you show up a week ago start playin' Three Card Monte with my head. Want you *gone*, Sonny! *(Continues circling his fists.)* Givin' ya three t'make dust; comin' out on the count o'three. One— *(Rises, moving to his corner of the "ring".)* (. . .)

Sound of the bell I'm comin' out. *You* won't hear it, but I *will. Two*— (. . .)

Dropped Billy D'Amato in the sixth round with both eyes swole shut. I just keep punchin' till I hear crunchin'. *Three*! (. . .)

OK, comin' out, comin' out; comin' at ya, boy, comin' at ya'— (. . .)

Prepare yourself, Mister, prepare yourself, get your—

(Midge suddenly lunges, bumping against the bench, stumbling—he struggles to keep his balance, grabbing desperately at the air—then falls flat on his back in the path. He lies there silently for several moments. Quietly, frightened.)

Oh, shit . . .

I'm Not Rappaport

Herb Gardner

Play
60+
Seriocomic

Nat accuses his concerned daughter, whom he calls Mrs. Gelber, of over-protectiveness.

You do frighten me, Mrs. Gelber. You do frighten me, you know. I'm afraid of what you'll do out of what you think is love. Coming to the Fountain once a week—it's not stopping me from talking; that's not so bad. It's the test questions. (. . .)

The test questions to see if I'm too old. *(Taps his head.)* Checking on the arteries. "Do you remember what you did yesterday, Dad?" "Tell me what you had for lunch today, Dad?" One wrong answer you'll wrap me in a deck chair and mail me to Florida; two mistakes you'll put me in a home for the forgettable. I know this. My greatest fear is that someday soon I will wake up silly, that time will take my brain and you will take me. That you will put me in a place, a home—or worse, your house. Siberia in Great Neck. Very little frightens me, as you know; just that. Only what you will do.

I'm Not Rappaport
Herb Gardner

Play
60+
Seriocomic

Midge was violently mugged in the park by a thug wearing a cowboy hat. In the retelling to Nat, whom he holds somewhat responsible, Midge makes himself into a hero.

'Nother thing—I ain't no General Custer. Way I heard it, the General got wiped out. Well, not *this* boy. Shit, wasn't for a lucky left jab I near blew that Cowboy away. *(Takes a small piece of buckskin fringe from his pocket.)*

See this? Small piece of that Cowboy is what it is. His jacket, anyways. Near took a good slice outa that boy, 'fore he dropped me. *(Leans back on the bench, smiling.)*

Know what I seen in the hospital every night, fronta my bed? I seen that Cowboy's eyes, them scared eyes, them big chicken eyes when my weapon come out. That was one, surprised, frozen-solid, near-shitless Cowboy. Dude didn't know what happened. Dude figured he had me on the ropes, out come my weapon and he turn stone. Lord, even eyes like mine I seen his eyes, they got that big lookin' at me. Yeah, yeah, he seen me, all right, he seen me; gonna be a while 'fore he mess with this alley cat again. *(Studying the piece of buckskin.)* Must be a way to frame a thing like this . . .

Impossible Marriage
Beth Henley

Play
20s
Seriocomic

Sydney Lunt, bespectacled and bearded, precisely relates the closest he's come to love.

There was this one girl I liked. We would chat and talk about ice cream selection. She worked behind the counter and offered me unlimited free samples in small midget spoons. Often I couldn't make a decision, or up my mind, and would ask for her recommendation. Her preference. I would put it to her like this, "Which flavor would you get?" I always enjoyed whatever she selected or chose, until one day she picked Pistachio. I wasn't pleased with it. It wasn't up my alley. I told her this and she gave me a new cone. The Rocky Road. She took the Pistachio from me, threw it in a canister, and said I was not to pay her for it. I knew she couldn't be giving out free cones. I was aware the price of the second cone would be deducted from her small wages. So I left money for it. The cone. Too much money really, but I could not stand to wait for change. I never came back, of course, because it may have been an uncomfortable situation. Anyway, it could never have been the same.

The Interview
James Thurber

Essay
58
Seriocomic

A reporter interviews a famous writer, a prodigious wordsmith, and self-proclaimed maniac. The reporter has just complimented the writer on his house.

Everybody says that. Everybody says it's a wonderful place, to which I used to reply "Thank you," or "I'm glad you think so," or "Yes, it is, isn't it?" At fifty-eight, Price, I say what I know. I say that you and the others are, by God, debasing the word "wonderful." This bleak prospect is no more wonderful than a frozen shirt. Even in full summer it's no more wonderful than an unfrozen shirt. I will give you the synonyms for "wonderful"—wondrous, miraculous, prodigious, astonishing, amazing, phenomenal, unique, curious, strange. I looked them up an hour ago, because I knew you would say this a wonderful place. Apply any of those words to that dahlia stalk down there. (. . .)

I have known only a few wonderful things in my fifty-eight years. They are easy to enumerate, since I have been practicing up to toss them off to you causally: the body of a woman, the works of a watch, the verses of Keats, the structure of the hyacinth, the devotion of the dog. (. . .)

Don't take the chair by the fire. That's mine. (. . .)

The Interview
James Thurber

Essay
58
Comic

Sent by Mr. Hammer, his editor, a reporter interviews a famous writer, a prodigious wordsmith, and self-proclaimed maniac.

Make us both a drink. That's a bar over there. (. . .) Easy on the soda. Martha will raise hell when she finds me drinking. Just bow at her and grin. (. . .)

What is this [editor] Hammer like? No, let me tell you. He says "remotely resembles," he says "flashes of insight." He begins, by God, sentences with "moreover." I had an English teacher who began sentences with "too." "Too, there are other factors to be considered." (. . .) This English teacher started every class by saying, "None of us can write." Hadn't been for that man, I would have gone into real estate—subdivisions, opening up suburbs, and so on. But he was a challenge. You can say my memoirs will be called *I Didn't Want to Write.* (. . .) I'll have to see a proof. I'll have to see a proof of your article. Have you noticed that everybody says everything twice? They say everything twice. "Yes, they do," you'll say. "Yes, they do." Only contribution I've made to literature is the discovery of the duplicate statement. "How the hell are you, Bill?" a guy will say. "How the hell are you, anyway?" "Fine," Bill will say. "Just fine." (. . .)

My memory is beginning to slip, but if you print that, I'll sue Hammer's pants off.

Jonathan Bailey's Out-of-Office Auto-Responder for 12 September, 2003

Wells Oliver

Short Story
30s+
Comic

While recording his outgoing message, a professional recruitment manager loses his professionalism.

I am currently out of the office and may return on the 19th of September, or I may not. I will be periodically checking e-mail, while lamenting my marriage and drinking heavily. I may check voicemail if the tremors permit. (. . .)

If you need immediate assistance—and likely you do, as everything is an emergency with you people—you may contact Jim Reading in Accounting, that ungrateful bastard. His extension escapes me but I am sure you are a resourceful individual—after all, you work in this fine and lauded company—and can therefore focus all of your well-honed skills upon finding it. I believe that Susan in Reception can assist you with the endeavor if she is sober. Do not let the abundance of chewing gum fool you. I have been watching her studiously and can assure you the wagon has left her far far behind. I only hope you can understand Jim through his god-awful lisp and mangling of the Queen's English and constant stuttering. I know I cannot. (. . .)

In conclusion, I urge you to contact me upon my return to the workplace. Feel free to drop by my office without notification or flag me down in the hallways with a friendly jerk on the collar. You deserve my full attention.

Kinnikinic
Roger Nieboer

Play
20-30
Seriocomic

Bobby, a blue-collar guy, recalls a rare moment of artistic achievement.

Like in high school. My choir director, Mr. Nelson, chubby little sucker that he was. Tenor. He was a tenor and I was a bass. That was part of it, I guess. Anyway, he got sick one winter and he had to stay outta school for about a week 'cuz he had to have this cyst thing cut off the end of his ass or something. He got the silly thing in the first place from sittin' on his ass all the time anyway. That's my theory. Anyway, he missed about two weeks. (. . .) [S]o we had study hall. Now all this amounted to was the basses beatin' the piss outta the tenors. Anyway, we never sang a lick. I thought, hell, I'd rather sing. So, I went up there, in front of everybody, and sorta took over. I stood up there and said, take out *Tu Pau Pe Rum,* and they did. Then I gave 'em their pitches off the pitch pipe, an' I raised my arms, just like ol' Mr. Nelson did, and I started 'em, and they sang. It wasn't too good, but it was OK. I stopped 'em and they stopped. And I talked to 'em 'bout crescendo an' told 'em to pretend they were in a cathedral. A big tall cathedral with just a little bit of light streamin' in, 'cuz that's what Mr. Nelson always told us, even though none of us had ever been in a cathedral before, except Vivian Robillard, 'cuz she still had a grandma who lived in France somewhere. Anyway, we tried it again and it sounded a little better. Well, we worked like that for two whole weeks, an' when Mr. Nelson came back from the hospital I told 'em we wanted to do something for 'em. A surprise. We wanted to do *Tu Pau Pe Rum*. That was our hardest song. Well, we did it for 'em . . . an' we did it really, really good. (*Pause.*) An' ol' Mr. Nelson jus' sat there, with his sore ol' ass all cut up an' restin' on a big pillow from the sick room. He jus' sat there for a minute an' said, "Bobby, I thought all you could do was change a muffler on a fifty-eight."

Land of Nod
Cathy Camper

Novel
17
Seriocomic

Cal and Owen are two runaway boys in a relationship. Cal is explaining to Owen for the first time what it was like growing up with ten siblings.

When I was growing up, I had five older brothers, and we all had to share two beds and one room (. .), I was the youngest boy, so if I didn't stake a claim to a corner of the bed in time, I'd end up sleeping on the floor. And sometimes I'd sleep upside down, because even if their feet were in my face, at least I'd kinda have my own space. (. . .)

The other thing was, we all had little cubbies with our names on 'em, and when my mom got around to it, she'd put each of our clean underwear and socks in the cubbies (. . .). But she hardly ever got around to it, I mean, with ten kids, it was just never ending. Half the time when I'd get up for school, I didn't have any underwear, so I'd just swipe some of Duane's or Brad's, or whoever's. But then, then I'd have to spend all day trying to ditch out on them in school, 'cuz if my brothers ever saw me, they'd sneak up behind me and yank the elastic of my underwear up, to check the tag and see if it was theirs or not. It'd be like, a total snuggie, plus if they caught me they'd box my ears, and it hurt!! (. . .) But then, of course, there was the other nasty shit they did to me, like I'd wake up with a pillow over my face, being smothered. I'd try to fight them off, but what can you do when they're so much bigger they can lift you off the ground with one arm? And they'd beat the shit outta me if I ratted them out to my folks. I finally figured out the best strategy was to go all limp like I'd fainted, then they'd get bored and I could run to the bathroom and lock the door.

The Last Word

Gus Edwards

Original Monologue
30s
Dramatic

A man tries to shake sense into a friend.

I listen to you, Man, and sometimes I begin to think that maybe we come from two different worlds. I mean we grew up together and all, but still we so far apart in the way we think (. . .). Don't you know that the sisters hate us? We is the enemy, man. (. . .)

You tell a sister one thing, she gon' tell you it's another. You tell her right, she gon' tell you it's wrong. (. . .) So getting yourself upset over what Jonelle says or how the woman is acting to me is dumb. (. . .) You worrying about the enemy when all the enemy is concerned about is how to see you dead or break you so bad that even your best friends wouldn't recognize you. If that's what you want, then go on. Drink up all the liquor in this place and smoke all the stuff that man in the back room is selling. But don't say I didn't warn you. And when you find yourself in that deep dark hole looking up, don't call me, cause I ain't gon' be around. This is my last word to you . . .

Lather, Rinse, Repeat

David Rakoff •

Short Story
30s+
Comic

A part-time actor is aware of his "type."

On the rare occasions when I find myself at an audition, it is generally to play one of two character archetypes: Jewy McHebrew or Fudgy McPacker. Jewy McHebrew is usually a fast-talking yet-beset-with-concern Talmudic sort, whose rapid-fire delivery, questioning answers, and dentated final consonants speak to the intellectual grappling and general worry that is so characteristic of the Chosen People, the People of the Book. Jewy gets to say things like, "Papa, I can't believe it. You sold the store?" or "And so we eat the bitter herbs? Why? Becauuuuse, it is to remember the bitterness of our enslavement in Egypt!"

Fudgy, on the other hand, can be many people: there is the phlegmatically imperious, supercilious salesman/concierge/executive assistant, who generally has lines like "We're not carrying that this season, I'm sorry. Next!" There's also best friend/next-door neighbor Fudgy, who is forever barging in to display his laughable sexuality by, say, wearing a Carmen Miranda hat, when he's not dispensing clear-eyed advice on matters of the heart. He is America's sweetheart; a harmless queen the whole country can love, with his constant refrains of "Did someone say swim team?" or "Can't you see that he's in love with you, kiddo? Just tell him."

There are, of course, hybrids and permutations. Today's part, for example, is a little bit of Secular Humanist Jewy McHebrew crossed with Cell Phone Schmuck Jewy McHebrew. I am playing, in short, an agent.

LGA-ORD
Ian Frazier

Essay
20s-30s
Comic

This is your captain speaking.

Extinguish the light extinguish the light I have extinguished the No Smoking light so you are free to move about the cabin have a good cry hang yourselves get an erection who knows however we do ask that while you're in your seats you keep your belts lightly fastened in case we encounter any choppy air or the end we've prayed for past time remembering our flying time from New York to Chicago is two hours and fifteen minutes the time of the dark journey of our existence is not revealed, you cry no you *pray* for a flight attendant you pray for a flight attendant a flight attendant comes now cry with reading material if you care to purchase a cocktail.

A cocktail?

If you care to purchase a piece of carrot, a stinking turnip, a bit of grit our flight attendants will be along to see that you know how to move out of this airplane fast and use seat lower back cushion for flotation those of you on the right side of the aircraft ought to be able to see New York's Finger Lakes region that's Lake Canandaigua closest to us those of you on the left side of the aircraft will only see the vastness of eternal emptiness without end. (. . .)

When we deplane I'll weep for happiness.

Like a Light Bulb
Antay Bilgutay

Play
Early 40s
Seriocomic

Chris has left his partner Larry to be a tour guide at the
Hoover Dam. Larry has just come to Nevada to confront him.

Who says I wasn't in it for life? Even if you're jaded and cynical
and cold, you don't spend years of your life living with someone, loving someone, waiting for the day it will end. You live.
You love. You find the small happinesses of your lives together,
and they can nourish you for a long time. But I tell you, when
it stops working, you know. It happens abruptly, the way a
light bulb goes out. And like it happens with a light bulb, you
fumble around in the dark for a while. You take out the bulb
and you shake it around. Is it really out? You don't want to
believe that your bulb could just stop like that. You hold it up
to your ear. Yeah, there's that little ringing sound. It's dead.
And for a while, you mourn the bulb that had shared its light
with you for so long. But you can't just sit there in the dark
forever. (. . .)

People don't always leave because they have a reason to go,
you know. Sometimes they leave because they've run out of reasons to stay.

The Line Forms in My Rear
Mark Saunders

Play
40-50
Comic

Mr. Talbot, a stressed-out rapid talker, takes his own blood pressure.

My second marriage ended in divorce six months ago. Good riddance, I say. She got it all, even the fuck-lousy dog. I got the crappy four-door American car with 100,000 miles on the same engine and dual-tone rust for a paint job. I'm losing hair like a Mexican Chihuahua. My rent is going up next week, again. My job sucks big time. We've had eight layoffs in ten months, almost one a month. How's that for a career path? If you stay there long enough they lay you off. Guaranteed. I'm probably next. I know I'm in someone's crosshairs. They're sniping employees off one by one. It's like the goddamn Soviet Union. One day you have someone in the cube next to you, the next day all his things are in a box, his screen's dark, and— pfffffttt—he's gone. No traces. As if he didn't even exist, ever. Wiped clean. Our CEO, now there's a piece of work, he keeps telling us "sacrifices must be made, sacrifices must be made." Then, BOOM. Another layoff, another human sacrifice. We're like Aztecs or Mayans or one of those primitive cultures where they cut open your heart so the rains will come.

Blood pressure is a little high.

Long Day's Journey into Night

Eugene O'Neill

Play
24
Dramatic

Edmund has been diagnosed with tuberculosis. Here, he walks on the beach alone after a fight with his father.

The fog was where I wanted to be. Halfway down the path you can't see this house. You'd never know it was here. Or any of the other places down the avenue. I couldn't see but a few feet ahead. I didn't meet a soul. Everything looked and sounded so unreal. Nothing was what it is. That's what I wanted—to be alone with myself in another world where truth is untrue and life can hide from itself. Out beyond the harbor, where the road runs along the beach, I even lost the feeling of being on land. The fog and the sea seemed part of each other. It was like walking on the bottom of the sea. As if I had drowned long ago. As if I was a ghost belonging to the fog, and the fog was the ghost of the sea. It felt damned peaceful to be nothing more than a ghost within a ghost. *(He sees his father staring at him with mingled worry and irritated disapproval. He grins mockingly.)* Don't look at me as if I'd gone nutty. I'm talking sense. Who wants to see life as it is, if they can help it? It's the three Gorgons in one. You look in their faces and turn to stone. Or it's Pan. You see him and you—that is, inside—and you have to go on living as a ghost.

Looking for Our Town
Henry W. Kimmel

Play
40+
Seriocomic

A Man goes to the theater to see a revival of Our Town *with Spalding Gray and is caught in the middle of the action. A lot has changed in* Our Town, *but the message remains the same. This monologue, by the Stage Manager, comes at the end of the play.*

Welcome back to Our Town. (. . .) It's fifteen years later and things have changed quite a bit in Grovers Corner. The Webbs' house was torn down and is now a subdivision of fifteen single-family homes. The Gibbs' home has been re-zoned for mixed use, (. . .) and the Main Street in Grovers Corner is now a strip of shopping centers (. . .). Businesses come and go, and no one notices. I'd take you over to the cemetery but even the ghosts have become strangers. The older families have moved away, not just scattered across New England, but the entire world. You still might see someone from the Warner family, but the Constable, he had to go out of town for sensitivity training. And the Newsome family, I'd rather not even bring them up. Each is on some kind of prescribed medicine, some necessary and some not, except for the youngest child—whose name I can't mention for legal reasons—who is now hooked on heroin. It's tough living in the suburbs, but my message remains the same: Even if you don't have kids, you should buy real estate in an area with a good public school if you hope to increase the equity in your house . . . (*To the MAN.*) You're not writing any of this down.

Love Is the Cookie
Antay Bilgutay

Play
34
Seriocomic

Todd has been dating Joey for nine weeks. They have just had a marvelous date, which moves Todd to express feelings for Joey for the first time.

You read *Martha Stewart Living*, right? You know how some of her recipes are impossible. Like, say she's got a fancy cookie recipe. You can never find *all* the ingredients exactly: car- damom, pine nuts, bitter Belgian chocolate, and butter from sheep's milk. You know? Where do you find this stuff? (. . .) [Y]ou can't go from store to store forever; you've got to bake the damn cookies. So you substitute. (. . .) You make the cookies with what you've got. (. . .) Hershey's kisses. Parkay. And when the cookies come out of the oven, they're fine, but they don't blow you away. They're just another kind of cookie.
(. . .) How do I explain this? Shit. I've dated a lot. OK, not a lot, but I've dated enough. And (. . .) when you say, "I love you," that's the cookie that you baked with what you could find at the other person's store. (. . .) [M]aybe it tastes OK, but it's not extraordinary. It's not the cookie that Martha led you to expect (. . .) Then one day, you find this amazing gourmet grocery that has all the ingredients you're looking for in one place. Sheep milk butter and all, and suddenly, you're able to make that cookie like it was meant to be. It comes out of the oven and it smells better, it looks better, and it tastes like nothing you've ever had before. What I'm trying to say is, you're my specialty store. I love you.

Love's Lumberings Remembered

Dawson Moore

Play
20-30s
Seriocomic

After not seeing her for over a year, Bryson runs into the girl of his dreams at an ATM. When she rips into him for not calling her back, he explains himself.

(Softly.) You know when you got me? It was when you and I were leaving, and we both looked at the leftover piece and a half of pizza and felt guilty that we weren't getting it "to go," that we were leaving that many mushrooms and that much cheese. At the bar, you brushed your knee up against mine and let it sit there. You brought our faces close together, whispering words that were meant just for me . . . I've read that those are signs. Signals that you are sending me. Empirically, I know this. But then I turned into Frankenstein's Romantic, lurching about and causing havoc. I know I remember getting us lost on the way there, but please tell me that smashing your glass into your teeth is just my memory embellishing things? Did I really spill my drink all over you, accidentally grab your breast on the dance floor, karaoke Elvis Costello? Of course I fell in love with you: We talked about believing in the paranormal without being embarrassed. Exchanged childhood stories, and stories with knives and danger and ghost grandmothers hurling us from cars. OK, that was just your story, but it was a pretty great story. But I couldn't pick up the phone. It weighed ten thousand pounds. *(Pause.)* And the weight I've been carrying for fourteen months has only gotten heavier by the day.

Mac-Blank, or the Most Evil Return of the Weird Witches, Three

Sean Wagner

Play
Early 30s
Dramatic

Charlie recounts a visit from an ancestor.

Head hurts.

I had a dream—a horrible, horrible dream . . . I shut my eyes, shifted my pillow, and I saw the end of my life—the end of all life. Blank as a film projection screen. Dead silent. I saw this imprint face, this . . . Shroud of Turin old man hovering out of the blankness and slowly dissipating. I thought "There's God, and there he goes."

So I tugged at the nothing, ran along the nothing, and I started crying after it, and tearing it, and pleading with it (. . .). But he might not have heard . . . might've chose not to. And pretty soon it was only me. Me and nothing, starting to disappear myself.

I woke up . . . and I could not console myself. I ran downstairs only half awake . . . I had to check in the bathroom mirror to make sure my face, my hands were still there. I ducked into each room, seeing if just one had remained blank; if there was still a smudge of it left on the coffee table—anything. I sat there, in that lounge chair, waiting for the fright to leave my hands—they were shaking pretty bad, see. My mind had on it an image of what eternity would look like . . . the more I tried to ignore it, the harder that little tin-type image was pressed. Inconsolable. I mean, *nothing.* I tell you, I'd rather not know than know this.

Mandelstam
Don Nigro

Play
47
Dramatic

Mandelstam, a great Russian poet, has died in Stalin's camps, but he returns to encourage his friend Pasternak to get on with his work despite everything.

Sometimes it seems as if everything is lost, but I think perhaps nothing has ever really been lost. It's just been mislaid. Just before I died, they moved me to another cell, a horrible stink-hole, but with a little window way at the top, and a bit of sunlight would shine in the window in the mornings, and slant down onto the wall of the cell, and I woke up one morning, and looked at that wall, and saw something written there, carved into the stone, and I couldn't quite make it out at first, but it seemed oddly familiar, so I went over to get a closer look, and I realized that it was a line from one of my poems. I don't know who carved it there, or when, or what happened to him, but there it was, carved on the wall of that hideous dungeon at the end of the world, a line from a poem I had written. Somebody remembered and wrote it down to give as a gift before they died. And I looked at that wall, and mumbled the words to myself, and I was, for that moment, absurdly happy.

Marcus Is Walking
Joan Ackermann

Play
20s–early 30s
Comic

Henry does his best to express his deep love for Lisa.

You know I'm normally pretty witty, my friends think I'm
funny, but when I'm with you my, I just, my tongue gets ship-
wrecked on my teeth. I have to say that it's not entirely *pleasant*
being so completely uncontrollably smitten by you. There's
actually quite a bit of pain involved that . . . a *lot* of pain I
can't do much about, but . . . Lisa, you touch something so
deep in me . . . I felt it the instant I met you, I had to run out of
the room. Your voice, your language, these phrases you come
up with—"loaded for bear," "boardinghouse reach" when you
reached across me in the conference room for pizza, "boardinghouse reach" I love that, I just . . . how you talk, your eyes,
your handwriting. Physically, I find you incredibly sexy but
that's the least of it . . . I love watching you watch things, I do,
I could watch you watching things forever . . . your sense
of . . . I'm babbling I know not very likely making much
but . . . if I can just at least try to express . . . No one has ever
made me feel the way that you do. I know, I realize it's *my*
problem, I'm not dumping all this on you, I'm the one who has
to deal with it, but I *am* in love with you. *(Pause.)* I guess we
should go.

Marshall
Rob Matsushita

Radio Play
30s
Comic

Marshall has agreed to help his buddy with a scheme to win back his girlfriend.

Well, I'm not sure what it is you want me to do.

I really don't think this is what's gonna make her talk to you.

No, I don't, in fact, knowing what I know of her, I can predict a major lawsuit.

And what am I supposed to do with the grappling hook?

Yeah.

OK, you see these scars?

You know what they're from, right?

They're from high school gym.

They're rope burns.

Now, that was when I was in my prime (such as it was) and when I was forty pounds lighter.

What makes you think I could—no, no.

You're insane.

No. No. No.

No, wait, don't walk away.

I have other questions.

OK.

What's the pig for?

No, seriously. What the hell is the live pig for?

I didn't ask where you got it, I asked—

OK, the grappling hook is to get into the building, and the tear gas is for our escape, and the fake police siren is to confuse the cops, and the birthday cake is Plan B, but what's the live pig for?

What?

A luau?

You know, I'm reasonably sure that this whole idea isn't about love anymore.

OK.

Grab the pig. I need to be home by at least two or what's happening to you is gonna happen to me.

Marshall
Diana Amsterdam

Original Monologue
20s
Comic

The drummer for the PlasterJammers begins to come out of his shell.

Anyway she comes right up to me and I'm thinking, is she blind? Because you know I'm not quite up to the level of the other guys, they are, well everyone knows they're like your really hot dudes and they make girls go nuts, yeah they do, I see it when we're playing, sometimes Zito will go over to the edge of the stage and he'll like let his sweat his actual perspiration like drip onto the girls in the pit? And they'll scream like they've just been blessed with the blood of friggin Christ, trust me, if I tried something like that? They girls'd be screaming like a pig had peed on 'em; but this girl, this girl in the bar? She comes right over to me, she sits down and she says, Don't I know you? And I'm looking at her and I'm running through high school, nope, junior high, nope, my town's marching band, nope, when she says, You're in the PlasterJammers aren't you, and I says, yeah, I'm the guy they hide in the back behind the drums and she says, listen I've heard about you. And I'm like: You've heard about me, what've you heard about but before I can even finish the thought, she's saying, I heard you're gay and I'm like: gay!! But I'm speechless because would a self-respecting queer especially one who has to show his arms all the time let himself get this friggin fat? But before I can say anything she's like, But I know you're not and I'm thinking, she heard I'm gay but she knows I'm not this girl is way ahead of me and I'm just about to ask How'd you know that? When she says, I see how you look at girls out of the corner of your eye but you're afraid to go after them because you think you're fat and ugly, but Hello, she says it in that girly-girl way, Hello, there are girls who like their men fat and ugly (. . .)

Master Harold and the Boys
Athol Fugard

Play
60+
Dramatic

*South Africa, 1950. Sam and Willie, both black men, work for
Hally's father, a white man. After sharing an easy camaraderie,
the boy Hally tells a cruel joke in which the punch line
describes "a nigger's arse" as being "fair." Sam's shocking
response spurs a violent confrontation.*

It's me you're after. You should just have said "Sam's arse" . . .
because that's the one you're trying to kick. Anyway, how do
you know it's not fair? You're never seen it. Do you want to?
*(Drops his trousers and underpants and presents his backside
for HALLY'S inspection.)*
     Have a good look. A real Basuto arse . . . which is about as
nigger as they can come. Satisfied? *(Trousers up.)* Now you can
make your dad even happier when you go home tonight. Tell
him I showed you my arse and he is quite right. It's not fair.
And if it will give him an even better laugh next time, I'll also
let him have a look. (. . .) *(SAM stops and looks expectantly
at the boy. HALLY spits in his face. A long and heartfelt groan
from WILLIE. For a few seconds SAM doesn't move.)*
     Ja, well, you've done it . . . Master Harold. Yes, I'll start
calling you that from now on. It won't be difficult anymore.
You've hurt yourself, Master Harold. I saw it coming. I warned
you, but you wouldn't listen. You've just hurt yourself bad.
And you're a coward, Master Harold. The face you should be
spitting in is your father's . . . (. . .)

Maui

Mike Albo

Original Monologue
30s
Comic

Mike's recent memories of working in the lap of consumerism catapults him back into the moment.

Have you ever worked in the Conde Nast Building? I was there all last year working at this new shopping magazine for men. Part of a new generation of magazines that are designed to help us decide what the hell to buy as we swim in our engorged mountain of consumer crap. I seriously just left there, like two months ago. (. . .) I was an editor. Coming up with copy like: "Wrap a patterned cravat around your neck instead of your usual dark variety and your basic sober suit suddenly has a social life!"

I wish I could get on my high Rage-Against-the-Machine horse and say I hated the job, but I didn't. I loved it. It takes intense haiku concentration to sit there hour after hour after hour and refine the perfect four-word description for a pair of Paul Smith sterling silver cufflinks, or a Helmut Lang herringbone Crombie Coat, or the perfect sentence to introduce an article about buying the perfect belt: Use these Belts tips for your Belts! (no . . .) Strap On These Belt Tips! (no . . . .) With These Tips, Buying a Perfect Belt is a Cinch! Ha! . . . phew . . .

Extension 2771 . . . Hi Ann! How are you! I know, I'm so tired today tooooo . . . Oh my god there's pralines and cream in the cremalita in the cafeteria, let's go! Get in the elevator with the Conde crowd, all zippy and zipped up in their corduroy blazers and princess slippers and shawls and iPod heads and look up at the little convenient news screen installed in the sleek interior and read about an explosion in Iraq. "Oh my god! We are such a disgusting country! I hate us! Hi Cheryl! I like your jeans are they Earnest Sewn?" And then go back to my desk and write more headlines: "Beanies, Baby! Jean Mutation! Creased Lightning!" I'm having a nervous breakdown! (. . .)

So after a year I wore out my brain and left.

The Migrant Farmworker's Son

Silvia Gonzalez S.

Play
Late teen
Dramatic

Henry, son of a Mexican-American immigrant, is becoming "Americanized," much faster than his father, who longs to return to Mexico. Here, Henry responds to his father's attempt to maintain his abusive authority.

See, Dad, it was bound to happen. I got used to it. I got used to all the beatings. Ever wonder if that would happen? This is not how you get respect. If only I had brothers and sisters to share in this delightful activity. If only they'd been here to either take it with me, or help me in telling you how wrong you are in doing this. Ever since I was little I had to cover what you did to me. I had to have a smile on my face and pretend nothing happened. So no one would suspect. Never see my shame. Never let anyone know what happens in this house. Keep hitting me, Dad, if it makes you feel better. After all, this is your house. I am a snake in the grass for not understanding you. For being too young and stupid to know why you hurt. I will always remember the beatings with pity for you, because the scars of this will be a lot deeper for you.

Mijo
Michael Kearns

Play
20s-30s
Dramatic

Michael pleads with the mother of his lover to allow her son to die peacefully of AIDS.

Listen to your own sermon, Carmen: "Deliver us from evil." That's all I'm asking. I'm asking you to deliver your flesh and blood from evil. Deliver your baby from evil. Deliver your *mijo* from evil. He cannot see; he cannot hear; he cannot laugh—you must help him die. Don't you get it? That's why you're here, to deliver him from evil pain; deliver him from evil suffering; deliver him from evil torment; deliver him from this hell on earth. If you love him, you will deliver him. If you love him, you will release him. You don't know what loving someone is until you deliver them from evil. (. . .)

He loved candles. We'll place them around the bed. We'll clean him up—bathe every inch of him like you did when he was a little boy—in candlelight. *We* are going to deliver him from evil. Put him to sleep.

Miss Beautyman
Tim Cage

Original Monologue
30s+
Seriocomic

Bob, standing with a half-full jar of capers in his hand, remembers an old acquaintance.

When Dr. Beautyman died, she left a half-full jar of capers in her refrigerator.

As her house sitter, I'd pretty much left the capers alone, although I did help myself to the Welsh Rarebit in the freezer. It might have been in there for years and years and years—but I was a hungry graduate student.

I knew her only as *Miss* Beautyman. She was about 80 years old, never married—much more a Grand Lady than a grand-ma type—with a great old house and award-winning azaleas. After living in her house all summer and for most of fall semester, I'd discovered a thing or two about her. She'd written her dissertation on a poet or playwright I'd misheard as "Shakespeare" when I asked her about it.

I'd found her doctorate diploma hanging inside the closet of an extra bedroom. The closet door had a handwritten note: "Woollens—keep closed." I don't think I'd ever seen the word "Woollen" spelled with two Ls before that.

Anyway, I had no business in that closet, and as soon as I mentioned seeing her diploma, I realized I'd exposed myself as a bad house sitter and got all mortified. That's probably why I heard "Shakespeare." I'm sure I stammered something stupid, hoping it was witty, about *Merchant of Venice*.

Miss Beautyman's death—not in Venice, but just after she returned home—was caused by a stroke. That was almost twenty years ago.

I'm not sure how, or why, or where the other half went . . . but I find I've got this half-empty jar of capers in my fridge.

Mr. & Mrs. Hollywood
Barret O'Brien

Play
Late 40s
Dramatic

Alex is a movie star.

I never even wanted to be an actor. As a kid. A ballplayer. Always a ballplayer. I wish you could have seen me run, just once. I was so fast . . . That's movie running. That's not real. I pull back for movies, always have, camera can't keep up with me. Even back in college, during televised games, they'd have trouble keeping me in frame. I'd break left and they'd go right, have to cut to a wide shot. It became sort of a game. See if I could lose them. Peter would tell me later that he noticed that, the way I'd play for the cameras. And when *Super Sunday* came up for casting he immediately thought of me. Never acted in my life and there I was, memorizing scenes, hitting marks, pretending I knew what I was doing. Playing a football player made it, of course, possible. Anytime we were out on that field didn't matter that it wasn't a real game—as soon as my foot hits that turf I'm in control. Everything makes sense to me out there—the white lines, the first-down marker. Get the ball and haul ass. Someone in your path? Run 'em over. One of your teammates down? Leave 'em. All that exists is that end zone. Drive—score—win. That's why so many people responded to me in *Super Sunday*—wasn't acting yet, it was real.

My Buddy List
Kelly DuMar

Play
Late 30s
Seriocomic

Tripp, recently divorced from Cin, describes how he stays in long-distance touch with his ex-wife and teenage daughter, Tick, via instant messaging.

They're on my buddy list, so I know when Cin or Tick logs on. That's how we stay in touch. Tick IM's me when she gets home from school. Chats with me. Unloads about her day. She likes it 'cause I bitch back. If you think about it, we're dealing with the same crap. Aspiring writer/teenager. Looking for *acceptance*. But, what you get most days is rejection. Nobody gets who you really are. Like Cin. Cin never got me. My need to express myself. To experiment with our sex life. Didn't get that at all. But, I never wanted to break up over sex. She'll tell you it was all *my* fault. That I cheated on her. But, cybersex isn't cheating. It was my solution for staying together. Cybersex is safe sex. No pregnancies. No STD's. Nobody gets hurt. Cin didn't see it that way. *You're out of control!* she'd scream. But, I never lost control. I've been cutting way down, as a matter of fact. Gotta get my screenplay done! *(A beat.)* It's wacky, I know. All that time, when she was lying there, right in our own bed, I didn't want her. Isn't it ironic? I want her like crazy now! When I'm typing, I hear the door open, and I see Cin's logged on! It's like she's inviting me in! I get so hot I can't stand it. *(Sound of Internet door opening.)* Here she is!

My Father's Girlfriend
Irene Ziegler

Novel
25-30s
Dramatic

Clyde, a firefighter, talks about his job on a first date.

I guess you heard we got some knucklehead running around in Tiger Bay State Forest, setting fires. I sure hope I'm the one to catch the son of a bitch. Two minutes, just give me two minutes with the guy. He'll never start another fire when I get finished with him, I can promise you that.

See, what this guy doesn't get is that each time he torches a construction site, for whatever reason, he's putting lives in danger. I'm not talking about the fire, now, I'm talking about all the other things that can go wrong. All this stuff we use—repelling gear, forcible entry tools, safety belts, breathing apparatus, pike poles, bolt cutters, nozzles, fire extinguishers—that's all expensive stuff, and it will hurt you, snip your fingers off if you take your mind off what you're doing for even a second. Plus, those houses over there to Tiger Bay, they're not that far from other developments. One good gust of wind and we got a major evacuation to pull off on top of everything else. That twisted bastard doesn't think about any of that. He's just getting off on the control, the power, whatever it is his mommy didn't give him enough of—attention, I guess. I swear, even if it turns out to be a kid, I'm going to extract my pound of arsonist buttsteak before this thing is all over.

The Old Settler
John Henry Redwood

Play
29
Dramatic

Husband Withersoon has come to World War II Harlem from South Carolina to find his girlfriend, Lou Bessie Preston. He speaks to Miss Elizabeth who is allowing him to board in her house.

I've been up here for almost four days looking for Lou Bessie and I've seen a lot. I don't think we were meant to live on top of one another like people do up here. When I woke up in the mornings, these past few days, I used to feel low and I couldn't figure out why. Then when I got on my knees this morning to say my prayers, I tried to look up to heaven, and that's when it came to me. There ain't no windows in that room! Now, I don't mean to be talking bad about your house, Miss Elizabeth. You keep a nice, clean, comfortable house just like my mama used to. But, I can't open my eyes and see the light of day . . . see the sky. When you do look out of a window, you look into a wall or into somebody else's window. I don't hear no birds or crickets . . . don't see a tree or lightning bugs. There's no place to take off your shoes and feel the grass and dirt on your bare feet. No, Miss Elizabeth, just as soon as Lou Bessie and me get things straightened out, we're going back down home just like I planned.

The Oldest Living Graduate
Preston Jones

Play
40s
Dramatic

Floyd hurls bitter feelings, like weapons, at his father.

Quit tellin' me what ah can and can't have. Ah've looked after this family for seventeen years, seventeen years! ME, Dammit, not you. Now, by God, from now on what ah say goes. That, Colonel, is an order and that is a fact! And to hell with Franklin. I'm sick of hearin' about him. You've stuck him down my throat ever since we were boys. Your precious damned Franklin. You know what Franklin was, you really want to know? He was a stuck-up, smarty-assed twirp! My beloved big brother. My first day in high school he sicked some of his buddies on me and they took my pants off in front of the whole school. I was layin' there in the dirt, too dammed ashamed to move, and he was laffin', laffin' louder than all the rest. I hated his guts and you put him on a pedestal forty feet high. Franklin the star! Football, basketball, track, baseball. "The Bradleyville Flash," isn't that what ever'body called him? You wanna know somethin' else? When the old "Flash" bought it in that B-17 ah was happy, happy as hell, because ah knew that if he lived out the war and came home some kind of hero I could kiss my life good-bye.

Other People's Money
Jerry Sterner

Play
40s
Dramatic

Lawrence Garfinkle is an obese, well-groomed, cunning Wall Street "takeover artist" from the Bronx. Here he defends his career on the stock exchange.

Hey, no matter what—it's better than working at the post office. (. . .)

A lot better than working at the post office. It's the best there is. Like in the old westerns, didn't everyone want to be a gunslinger? Didn't everyone want to be Butch Cassidy and the James Boys? There's just a few of us—us modern-day gunslingers. There's T. Boone and the Bass Brothers out of Texas. Irwin Jacobs out of Minneapolis. Would you believe a gunslinger named Irwin Jacobs? The Belzberg Boys up north in Canada. And here in New York we got Saul Steinberg and Ronald Perlman and Carl Icahn. *(Places his hand on his heart.)* Out of respect for the stupid a moment of silence for our gunned-down colleague Ivan Boesky. *(With a big smile.)* It's assholes like him that give assholes like us a bad name. And last, but not least, Garfinkle from the wilds of the Bronx. But instead of galloping in with a six-gun a-blazing in each hand, we're driven in, escorted by a herd of lawyers and investment bankers (. . .) But they quake just as hard. And they wind up just as dead. And it's legal. And it's exciting. And it's fun. *(Moves to desk.)* And the money ain't bad either. *(Sits at desk.)*

And every so often, every once in a while, we even wind up with the girl.

Other People's Money

Jerry Sterner

Play
40s
Seriocomic

Lawrence Garfinkle is an obese, well-groomed, cunning Wall Street "takeover artist" from the Bronx. Here he defends his career on the stock exchange.

Do you want to give a speech or do you want an answer? 'Cause the answer is not complicated. It's simple. I do it for the money. I don't need the money. I want the money. Shouldn't surprise you. Since when do needs and wants have anything to do with one another? (. . .) I *loooooove* money. I love money more than I love the things it can buy. And I love the things it can buy. You know why? Money is unconditional acceptance. It don't care whether I'm good or not, whether I snore or don't, which God I pray to— (. . .). There's only three things in this world that give that kind of unconditional acceptance—dogs, donuts, and money. Only money is better. It don't make you fat, and it don't shit all over the living room floor.

Our Lady of 121st Street
Stephen Adly Guirgis

Play
30s
Dramatic

Rooftop, a popular Los Angeles D. J., wants to reconcile with the love of his life.

I'm a make this call 'cuz I have to, but I need you to think on this till I get back: Ain't my fault about your husband, dass on you. And it ain't my fault 'bout your scorched-up heart—you married me juss like I married you. And I got no choice but to try and forgive myself for everything I done to you, 'cuz, what's the fuckin' alternative, Inez? I usta think there was some other option, some way 'round it, but there really ain't. I can try an' forgive myself, or, I can go jump off the GW—and dass it! I feel guilty 'bout a girl been dead fifteen years, and you? You angry at a boy—a boy, Inez—not me . . . Do I wish I had done it dif-ferent back then? Hell yeah. Even now, I'm tempted to take this conversation in another direction juss so I could get with you. And I could get with you if I worked my game right, don't tell me I couldn't 'cuz I'm a fuckin' professional—but what would be the point a that? I lost you—dass my cross. 'Cuz you was my royal. And I killed it. But if you wanna walk around all these years later still tryin' ta play dead, dass your waste, not mine . . . dass on you. I'm a make my call now.

Perfectly Cut Grass
Bill Nelson

Original Monologue
40s
Seriocomic

Brian opens the door of his house to greet Steve, whom he's been expecting.

Yes, I got your letter and I'm not gonna read it. (. . .) I know what's been going on. (. . .) My head's not in the dirt, for God's sake. And I know you want to confess, to clear the air, or get me to punch you, or something, but it won't make me feel better, all right? We've been best friends since KU, and Margaret and I—We've never had problems like this. Our whole marriage. (. . .) If you say it out loud, it makes it real, OK? The last sentence I'd ever want to read is, "Brian, please forgive me, I slept with your wife." IF that even happened. You've been around the house a lot lately, so what?

It's not even Margaret and me I'm thinking about. It's Amy. The number one thing in my life is to raise a happy daughter. She's lived nearly fourteen years in a happy home (. . .). Amy's an innocent girl and—I mean you know that; she adores you. (. . .)

Man, what's that? Don't cry! God, Amy'll hear you. God! All right! All right, I'll read it. I'll read it once then neither of us will mention this again. *(Opens letter, reads.)* "Brian, I hope you can forgive me, I slept with your daughter."

Philadelphia Cream Cheese

Jason Feifer

Essay
30s+
Comic

A sweet and embarrassing food memory.

My father and I used to eat Philadelphia Cream Cheese by the slice. We'd buy one of those bricks of cream cheese, the type wrapped in easily torn and obviously ineffective foil, and dig in with butter knives. Slice, gulp. Slice, gulp. The stuff was so slippery and smooth, so cool as it oozed down my throat, that I sometimes didn't chew. We laughed as we ate, our cream-cheese-covered teeth glowing and bulbous. It wasn't until seventh grade, when I mentioned this to a friend, that I discovered that the world does not eat cream cheese by the slice. In fact, the world thinks that eating cream cheese by the slice is disgusting. Who knew?

Phoenix
Don Nigro

Play
40
Seriocomic

Rutger, a German immigrant to the United States, is living in Phoenix, Arizona, in 1961 and running a bowling alley that his wife, Doris, inherited from her late husband. Rutger hates the vulgarity of American culture and has had it with his wife's hunger for emotional intimacy.

Doris, it's a beautiful day in the Valley of the Sun. It's warm outside, and it's nice and cool in our bowling alley. People will come and pay money to rent smelly shoes and roll heavy balls down long wooden alleys and knock down fat wooden pins, and this will, absurdly, make them happy. And we'll sell them drinks that will rot their teeth or destroy their brain cells, and rolled up weeds they can stick in their mouth and set on fire and breathe in toxic smoke that will rot their lungs, and food boiled in the melted fat of dead animals that will clog their arteries and destroy what little brain function they have left after watching television, and then at night we'll go home and screw like a couple of weasels. So be thankful for what you've got, Doris. A gigantic asteroid could strike the earth at any moment. A volcano could erupt all over you. You could be torn apart and devoured by a wild puma who has crept down from the Superstition Mountains. So enjoy what you've got while you've got it, and let me read this desperately stupid American newspaper in peace.

The Pleasure of My Company
Steve Martin

Novella
30s
Comic

The obsessive protagonist, a former code-breaker, analyzes his girlfriend's behavior.

I can cut a moment into quarters, then eighths, then et cetera, and I am able to analyze whether one bit of behavior truly follows another (. . .).

I couldn't make out what was troubling Clarissa because she's adept at being sunny. (. . .) Then something exciting happened. Her cell phone rang. It was exciting because what crossed her face ranged wildly on the map of human emotion. And oh, did I divide that moment up into millionths:

The phone rang.
She decided to ignore it.
She decided to answer it.
She decided to ignore it.
She decided to check caller-id.
She looked at the phone display.
She turned off the phone and continued speaking.

But the moment before turning off the phone broke down further into submoments:

She worried that it might be a specific person.
She saw that it was.
She turned off the phone with an angry snap.

But this submoment broke down into even more sub-submoments:

She grieved.
Pain shot through her like a lightning strike.

Portnoy's Complaint
Philip Roth

Novel
30+
Comic

New Jerseyite Alexander Portnoy explains to his therapist what it was like for him to visit a foreign land called Iowa.

Then there's an expression in English, "Good morning," or so I have been told; the phrase has never been of any particular use to me. (. . .) But suddenly, here in Iowa, in imitation of the local inhabitants, I am transformed into a veritable geyser of "good mornings." That's all anybody around that place knows how to say—they feel the sunshine on their faces, and it just sets off some sort of chemical reaction: Good *morning! Good* Morning! Good *morn*ing! Sung to half a dozen different tunes! Next they all start asking each other if they had "a good night's sleep." And asking me! Did I have a good night's sleep? I don't really know, I have to think—the question comes as something of a surprise. Did I Have A Good Night's Sleep? Why, yes! I think I did! Hey—did you? "Like a log," replies Mr. Campbell. And for the first time in my life I experience the full force of a simile. This man, who is a real estate broker and an alderman of the Davenport town council, says that he slept like a log, and I actually *see* a log. *I* get it! Motionless, heavy, *like a log!*

A Private Practise
Andrew Biss

Play
50-60s
Comic

Dr. Pecksniff, a rather unorthodox psychiatrist, has just learned of his patient's penchant for steamy romance novels.

Oh, my dear lady, if you could only hear yourself. You really have no idea what's happening to you, do you? Your weakness for manipulation is quite remarkable and I must tell you, you made a very wise decision in coming here to see me today. Very wise, indeed. It's the thin end of the wedge, you see. *(Pacing the room.)* Oh, I'm sure it begins harmlessly enough—a timid toe dipped oh-so-lightly into the suggestive waters of romantic fiction. But believe me, my dear, before you know it you'll be swimming in a sea of unimaginable filth and depravity. It's a disease, Mrs. Flagg, that tempts and torments even the most chaste and pure of heart. *(Leaning forward, forebodingly.)* You are on the edge, Mrs. Flagg—teetering. One push and you could spiral recklessly into a world of unending mental and physical abandonment. A condition so racked by depraved thoughts and vile-smelling activities that the very fiber of your existence will feel soiled. You'll look into the mirror one day and no longer see the lily-white splendour of all that is Mrs. Flagg looking back at you. Oh dear, no. I'm afraid all you'll see is the image of everything that you have become: a sweating, heaving mound of flesh, grunting and snorting like some repugnant farm animal. *(Beat.)* It's most unpleasant.

The Return to Morality
Jamie Pachino

Play
40s+
Comic

Armando le Becque, a huge publishing mogul, wheels around in his chair, holding a manuscript.

Brilliant! You hear me Brilliant! Haven't seen anything like it in ten years. We mass-produce. Huge campaign. Frontline, Nightline, Prime Time, Late Night, Tomorrow, Today. Good Morning America, here's your fucking wake-up call! And you! Look at you—sweet, young, scruffy, from the middle of nowhere. Still got your looks, your hair. You got a girl? You're single. He's single. (*Makes a note.*) Call Oprah. Charlie Rose. Low on ratings, but good on the resume. Screw Springer. We keep you clean. Up. Get you on Oprah with the blacks, Matthews with the environmentos, The View with those God-help-us feminists, and we roll. Get you a new suit. A press agent, a girl—an assistant—and . . . (*Looks.*) . . . maybe a personal trainer. And. We get it into stores by election time! By primaries!
(*Beeps the outside office.*)
Marge. Can we get something out by primaries? Before primaries? Then get me Simpson!
(*Back to ARTHUR.*)
This is beautiful. Where were you in the 80s?

Revelations
Heidi Decker

Play
25+
Comic

A young man discovers his problems aren't his fault.

There was a special on TV last night . . . it was about a modern day exorcism. They are really popular again. Who knew? The Catholic Church doesn't do them anymore . . . or, rarely, at least. Apparently they've had just too many PR problems.

So anyway, it seems to have been usurped by fundamentalist Christian preachers.

The point is, there was a story about this man . . . they interviewed him the day before the Big Exorcism. He described how he's been depressed a good portion of his life. He had an unhappy childhood, and difficulty with adult relationships. He suffers from insomnia, feels inadequate, lost. He has spent his life feeling empty, unfulfilled . . . always as if something is missing. Something is off, somehow.

He tried antidepressants, they didn't work. Therapy, no luck. Finally, one day, his pastor suggested that he see a specialist. A specialist in exorcism.

After a brief consultation, he is diagnosed as being possessed by a demon.

The man was thrilled. Relieved. Couldn't wait for the exorcism. Finally he had an answer. It all made sense now!

So I'm sitting there, as he's listing all of these symptoms . . . and I'm thinking, well, that's me, and that's me . . . that too, yup, that's me too. And then . . . it hits me.

I have a demon! Oh, what a relief.

I've decided to call him Larry.

Saturday Night
Jason Caldwell-Hughes

Original Monologue
30s+
Seriocomic

Charles, a usually law-abiding citizen, recounts the horrible consequences of a night out.

We were coming back from a party at the COUNTRY CLUB, for chrissakes. David handed me the keys. I had three glasses of wine, in no way felt impaired. Since the country club is in the, duh, country, I turned on my brights, you know, the headlights.

Ten blocks from home, I was pulled over. It seems it is illegal to drive with your brights on. Who knew? Oops, says I to the nice officer. So sorry. Didn't mean to do that.

"Have you been drinking, sir?" Lesson #1. Never answer "yes."

In the street, in front of ogling bystanders, I *rocked* on the thirty-second, one-legged stance. I was a crane, serene and solid. But on the heel-toe walk-and-pivot, I apparently looked like I'd recently had both hips replaced.

I am offered the breathalyzer. Confident, I accept. I mean, three glasses of wine. Come on.

The legal limit in Florida is .08. I blew .09 and some change.

At this point, David gets out of the Land Rover. He is told by Florida's finest to get back in the car. David wants to make sure I'm all right. He is surrounded by cops, he is worried. Again, he is told to get back in the car. Again, he insists he just wants to make sure I'm all right. One more round of orders and refusals, and boom. David is arrested for Drunk and Disorderly. I lunge for the officer who is "assisting" me to appeal for mercy. The next thing I know, my hands are behind my back and I have to pee so bad I'm turning yellow.

Lesson #2. When on your way to jail, don't ask the nice officer if you can stop at Wendy's to use the bathroom. Things can get ugly fast.

Scathed
Sean Muir

Play
20s
Comic

Sometimes, it's just hard to explain.

I'm just not. It's not that I'm an egomanic, or have some unquenchable sexual appetite or anything . . . It's that I . . . I can't stand breaking up . . . You know, it just hurts, so, the truth is that I'm not a one-girl guy. OK, say you're on one of those circus monocycle things, now say the wheel goes out, you're screwed right? You're out in the center ring on your face in the dirt and the fucking clown is just dancing around pointing at you. Well, let's say you're on a bicycle . . . Wheel goes out and it's going to take some work and some skill to keep going . . . but it's possible. You can lean back, ride on just one wheel, you might not be any Lance Armstrong, but you're moving. You get it? The wheels are like the girlfriends. So when a wheel goes out it's like losing a . . . OK now lets say you're on a tricycle, subways are out or something and you, you have to get to Battery Park immediately, you jump on the tricycle and you're screaming down Fifth Avenue and the tire goes out. But you don't have to worry because you still got two wheels left . . . well there you have the problem with the wheels not quite being lined up, so I guess it still would be kind of hard to balance but . . . God, I really need to think out these metaphors a little better.

scatsong

Ernest Slyman

Play
20+
Dramatic

We're talkin' jaaaaaaazz.

In a Jazz Club, on MacDougal Street,
The horns blow cool, crazy, wild, talking up God,
Jumping in your brain, naughty and nice.
Trumpets feeling lucky, clapping a great bell —
Our ears flung wide like pearly gates,
Cause jazz teach us how to live,
And you hear a child call,
Saxophone chirp, hiccup, fart
And crying, rocking back,
Wicked, big mouth Mama kissing her baby, laughing, running
up and down your spine,
Bebop biting off your ear again and again, sweet tomorrow,
Naked, large truths bursting in your brain, zombie-eyed, God's
secret out, everybody know
Jazz eats you up, spits out your bones, cause what you say
don't mean nothing,
And here come that bliss, sorrow, guilt, sin kicking, chirping as
one big sound
Plucks you right up out of your skull, throws you down a hole,
And the deafness roars, sings like an atomic bomb,
And you so gone happy, frenzy loving, mad fool,
You slap your dead daddy and start running around with Jesus,
Until everything good and sacred,

Sticks you in the belly with a knife, takes out your appendix
And waves it in the air, jiggly fish,
(. . .) And upstairs, the musicians lay down their riffs,
Swing like birds chirping up the dawn,
Till everything we hold dear jabbers
Gloriously singing scat, scat, whodat,
And an great big orange sunrise
Swoops down and yaps in our bones,
Hurl us toward the soft fleshy dark.

Separate the Man
From His Head

Michael Rothschild

Original Monologue
20+
Comic

*Coach, a bellicose figure in a Tom Landry-esque hat, is on
stage. He blows a whistle, then starts talking.*

Hustle up, ladies! Let's go. Take a knee and take a listen. I'm
not happy with what I saw on the football field today. (. . .)
[W]eak-ass hitting is not tolerated on this football team. When
you hit a man, HIT him! (. . .) You drop him like a wet sack
of crap and he knows he got dropped! Lower your shoulder
and lower the boom! BOOM! (. . .)

Defense, you don't just separate the man from the ball, you
separate the man from his HEAD! (. . .)

When I took this job they told me I couldn't coach the way
I used to. (. . .) They told me, (*In namby-pamby voice.*) "but
Coach, its only pee-wee football! They just want to have fun!"
I don't give a crap about that crap. You may only be eight years
old, but you still got a pair, right? Are you here to have fun and
drink juice boxes, or are you here to kill, destroy and win? (. . .)

I know it's tough. (. . .) Most of you can't bench your
weight. Hell, half of you can't tie your own shoes. But hitting
ain't about muscle. It's about how bad you want it. (. . .) It's
about the men you boys will become. (. . .) Do you want to
start on the right path, or on the path to smokin' dope and

being a mime? You kill a man today, you save your life tomorrow. Nobody who ever played football became an actor. 'Cept that fella' on *Webster*. But I digress.

Now let's throw 'em up for Jesus.

Shining Sea
Jonathan Dorf

Play
30s
Seriocomic

Candy is a squeegee man living in New York City, but the New York in which he lives is one in which there are now two rival Mayors, and the city is falling into chaos and civil war. He talks to Violet and Pac, his "family," a thirty-something woman and a young man just out of his teens.

When I was little, my Pops would make me go to bed at eight—we're talkin' when I was six, maybe seven—and as soon as I'd turn out the lights, he'd start mowin' the lawn. Crank up the floodlights and cart out the oldest working lawn mower in the history of the world. Needed a paint job, needed an oiling, needed a muffler in the worst way. Three times a week, eight o'clock: mow the lawn. Neighbors didn't mind too much in the summer—half of them were at the shore—but every other time of the year it was World War III. I'd stay up half the night, couldn't get the damn lawn mower sound outta' my head. Or I'd stay up listening to the people: them complaining at him, him screaming at them, them calling the cops, him screaming at the cops, the cops haulin' him off to cool down. Even on the nights he didn't mow, I'd still stay up, waiting for the sound—
      (There's the pop sound of gunfire, not so far away.)
      And then I start to sleep through it. I sleep through the mowing and the screaming and the sirens. Regular little log. Wake up from yet another good night's sleep at the age of nine to find my mom crying louder than a tribe of monkeys and my

Pops a former person. I use both hands to pull the knife out of his chest, then go back upstairs to squeeze in another hour. By the time I wake up, my mom is gone and the cops are there, and I'm sleepin' like the dead for the next thirty years.

(Beat.)

This pop pop pop's starting to fuck up my sleep again.

Sin, Sex & Cinema
Roger Nieboer

Play
20-30
Seriocomic

Harold recalls an incident from his adolescence.

Sister Georgette. Yeah, I think it was her who told me once, strictly off the record, that is *not* a part of our catechism lesson to be memorized word for word, swallowed, stashed in the brain and prepped for immediate regurgitation at a moment's notice. It was her who told us a story, in answer to one of Kevin Gullickson's hypothetical questions. He was always trying to put Sister Georgette on the spot with a grilling theological stumper, and this time he asked her what would happen if a priest fathered a child. And Sister Georgette sort of gasped and said that would never happen, and Kevin Gullickson said, well, just suppose it did. What would happen Sister? Suppose that like maybe this young priest, who was very reverently celibate, suppose that he had a nocturnal emission, and he woke up to smoke a cigarette and suppose the bed accidentally caught fire, so he threw the sheets out the window, into the swimming pool below where a girls' physical education class was learning the breast stroke, and suppose some of the gametes on the sheets worked their way through the water and into the uterine canal of one of the girls . . . What would happen Sister?

Small Domestic Acts
Joan Lipkin

Play
30s-40s
Dramatic

Frank has just had a fight with Sheila, the woman with whom he lives, about whose turn it was to make dinner.

She's always angry these days. I didn't know it when we were first together. Because she was sweet then. I guess we were both on good behavior. You know, polite. Asking which movie the other one wanted to see. And now, there is all this anger. I feel a little cheated. Like she is not the girl she made herself out to be. Sometimes, it scares the hell out of me. And the littlest things set her off. (. . .) Now, me? I'm just regular all the time. The same. What you see is what you get. *(Beat.)* (. . .) *(Beat.)* Most of the time, it's pretty good. I love sleeping with her and she does nice things for me sometimes. (. . .) Maureen, my last girlfriend? She never got angry. And she was pretty. I was never as hot for her like I am for Sheila, but it was OK. It was comfortable. We had the house and we had our friends and in the beginning, she used to bake all the time. Just like my mom. I'd come home and the house would smell like chocolate. But one day, she came home and said she wanted out. Just like that. I wanted to work it out. I even said I'd go see someone and I don't go in for that kind of bullshit. But she said it was too far gone. Too much had happened that she couldn't live with. So now, even though I don't understand it and it sometimes makes me crazy, I'll take Sheila's anger any day. Besides, with someone else, if it wasn't this, it would be something else.

Solitaire
Rosary O'Neill

Play
20s
Seriocomic

Gallery of the Dubonnet summer mansion, Pass Christian, Mississippi. Rooster Dubonnet, an artist with boyish charm, speaks to his mother.

(Chugs Jack Daniels.)
I have received an ancient legacy. Painting either brings you to the cocktail circuit or to God!

But I haven't reached HIM. I practice to get it right.

Dodging the predators. That isn't easy because the laws of the sea don't apply. Out there, predators have names: electric eel, swordfish, hammerhead shark. Sharks have survived for over 400 million year, prowling the earth before dinosaurs. Because of their successful design, sharks have changed little— Here, humans are slippery and perverse. You've got loved ones like red-bellied piranha hungering to extract your talent. Going into a frenzy for a drop of genius. A piranha's teeth snap like a steel jaw. You don't stop one by patting its head, Mother. I survive by keeping a low profile like a flatfish, pressed to the sea floor. I was born like a regular human, but my eyes have rolled atop my head from crawling along the bottom. It's easier for me to change me than for me to change you.

(Drinks and recalls a quote.)
Yeah I know I'm drunk and you're a bitch, but I'll be sober in the morning.

The Speed of Darkness

Steve Tesich

Play
18
Dramatic

In this opening monologue, Eddie sets the stage for a tragedy.

There was a family that lived here. I am almost tempted to say once upon a time, but it was only a little over a year ago. The father was a hero in this town. The mother was a mother. The daughter was Mary. Neither the inner structure of the atom nor the infinity of space is as mysterious to me as the living room of this house. Blood was spilled on the floor of this living room. Right there. You can't see it at night, but there is a huge mesa out there. It rises nearly fifteen hundred feet above the ground and there is still only a dirt road going to the top. It is hard for me to understand how anyone could sit in this living room and look out at that sight for fourteen years, knowing the crimes he had committed. The story of Joe and his family has been abandoned by everyone else in my town. Perhaps because I played a small part in that story, I can't seem to let go of it. The tragedy would have occurred without me, but I was, without knowing it at the time, the messenger who brought the news which caused it to unfold. The principals are all gone now. Only the messengers remain. The house has been for sale for over a year. They used to live right here.

The Speed of Darkness
Steve Tesich

Play
16-18
Seriocomic

Eddie, a high school senior, has issues. This is his answer to "And how're your mom and dad?"

The best that can be said is: Not bad at all . . . considering (. . .) that my dad's in real estate, that the real estate market is soft and Mom is hard, and the holy season is upon us . . . Holidays, especially the religious holidays, bring out the butcher in my mom and she hacks away at my dad in a most alarming way. She likes to recapitulate his life's accomplishments around this time of year. "Our breadwinner," she starts calling him. "Another Christmas with Mr. Jackpot!" Things like that. (. . .)

. . . when that story about the mesa project came on [the TV], my poor dad made the mistake of saying that he thought it was a bad idea to be building up there, ruining things. "Look who's talking about ruins!" My mom jumped all over him. And you see my dad, he has this thing about the holiday season and religious holidays in general. He can't defend himself during that time. He has to wait for the secular holidays to strike back. That means he'll have to wait until Martin Luther King's birthday before he unloads on her (. . .).

The Speed of Darkness
Steve Tesich

Play
40s
Dramatic

Lou, a homeless veteran of the Vietnam War, asks to hold Eddie and Mary's school project, a sack of soil representing a baby. Once the "baby" is in his arms, he breathes life into the illusion with heart-wrenching tenderness.

(. . .) There are . . . in this life . . . there are strange weights and loads. And if you have them, you feel lighter. And if you don't you feel burdened. The scientific community can't figure it out. I was once sitting on a park bench in Riverside Park in New York City when, out of nowhere, this little bird landed on my knee. What could a little bird weigh? Nothing. But it made me feel fifty pounds lighter. Made my spirits rise. This baby. Same thing.

(LOU clutches it closer to him, threatening to break down, but instead, he uses his own mood and transfers it to the baby. Turns his head aside and does a wonderful imitation of a baby crying. Mary is amused. Eddie is trying to be. Lou clowns around, alternating crying like a baby and then becoming the soothing voice of an adult.)

W-a-a-a! There, there. Don't cry. Wa-a-a! No, don't cry. Sshhh. Don't you worry, little baby. We're doing all we can to make sure the world's nice for you. Yes, we are. All we can. We won't let you down. Sssssh. (. . .) *(Rocks it lovingly.)* (. . .) It's waiting to see if I keep my word. Never promise a baby anything unless you plan to do it. They remember every word you tell them. (. . .)

Stuck Rubber Baby
Howard Cruse

Graphic Novel
Late 20s
Seriocomic

The time is 1963. Orley is a religious Southern man in his late twenties. His young brother-in-law Toland has been sleeping off the ravages of a night that included being arrested for public drunkenness. Toland has awakened to discover Orley kneeling by his bed in the dark, weeping and praying.

I'm sorry, Toland. I shouldn't of been in here with you asleep. I was intendin' to say a little bedside prayer . . . but then I just started cryin'.

That's right, pal. Be flip! Never act like there might be anything of importance goin' on in the mind of a dumb ol' guy that loves you.

What's buggin' me? The path you're showin' signs of headin' down. Drinkin' in bars . . . hangin' around with people that get arrested . . . it could end up with you goin' to Hell! Oh, I know that you're the last person who'd take that risk to heart. You think that Hell's some imaginary concept! But Hell is real! It's an actual place in the Universe. I don't want you to find that out the hard way. But if you don't take a careful look at the life you're leadin' . . . Please, Toland, think about what might be in store for you. Horrible torture that'll last forever and ever. There'll be no end to it, Toland, no relief from the agony. Smelly boils festerin' all over your body. Flames lickin' like acetylene torches at you while stingin' pus oozes from your pores an' trickles like a river of acid down every inch of your skin. An' there won't be anything your sister or I can do to help. We'll be in Heaven (Lord willin'), but it's hard to see how we can be very happy there, knowin' you're in the pit sufferin'.

(He is interrupted by another sarcastic remark. He shakes his head in frustration.)

Flippancy, flippancy! Cut right into my heart with your flippancy! Nothin' left for me to do but pray for you a hundred times harder, just to make up for the blindness that won't let you pray for yourself.

Stuck Rubber Baby

Howard Cruse

Graphic Novel
Early 20s
Dramatic

*The time is 1963. The speaker is Toland Polk, a southern
"good ol' boy" in his early twenties who, in a moment of crisis,
is baring his soul to his girlfriend. Having just confessed with
great shame that he fears he is gay, he goes on to share this
story.*

The spring I finished high school they held a picnic in honor of
the seniors. It was the same every year—half the class, it
seemed was paired off: boy, girl, boy, girl. Some of 'em were in
love, or felt like they were. A fair number knew they'd be sepa-
rated soon, what with college or goin' into the military.

They sat around on the grass, some of 'em holdin' hands, a
few practically neckin' right there in front of everybody. The
chaperons were careful to see that nothin' got out of hand. But
even so, they kept castin' tender, indulgent glances at all the
young couples, like it was so fuckin' wonderful that the plan of
nature was bein' fulfilled by these sweet, straight teenagers, all
moon-eyed an' horny.

An' I felt like shit! 'Cause I knew in my gut—as much as I
worked at not puttin' anything into words—that I would never
be part of that picture. I'd been born different, an' nobody was
ever gonna look at *me* an' think it was wonderful that *I* was in
love.

Suburban Redux
Andrew Biss

Play
20s
Dramatic

Tristram, a shy, awkward young man, has just been rebuffed by the high-spirited woman he adores.

No, no, it's quite alright. And it isn't self-pity, it—it's self-knowledge. I'm quite aware of who I am I'm quite aware that I've never had a—a particularly interesting or revealing thing to say or contribute in my entire life. I'm a decidedly dull individual, and it was stupid and vain of me to imagine you could regard me as anything else. But it's who I am. I don't wish to be dull. Who would? I can imagine nothing more wonderful than to be an object of fascination in the eyes of another. But no matter how I try it's not to be—not for me, at least. *(Beat.)* Oh, don't get me wrong—I—I'm not saying I don't find life interesting. I do. I find it immeasurably interesting, as I do people, and art, and music, and literature . . . and you. I think that must be why I love you a—and love being with you—you fill in the bits of me that are missing. When I'm with you I feel as though I am interesting and witty and clever. And I'm sure any number of psychologists would be happy to tell me that that's vicarious a—and weak and wrong of me, but you see . . . it makes me so very happy.

Take Out Taxi
Mike Albo

Original Monologue
30s
Comic

The agony of the first post-college job search.

(. . .) [H]ow to write the perfect cover letter: "Put your name exactly one-fifth down from the margin of the page, use action words like *utilize* or *implement* and never, never close the letter asking them to call you, instead always say "I hope to speak to YOU further about this position. I will call YOU next week to discuss it. Thank YOU for your time and consideration."

I had to move home after graduating into my old eighth grade stripe-y bedroom with its Far Out Facts magazines and Electronic Detective and my teeny tiny little stiff twin bed mattress with crackerjack pillowcases and old flaky scratch 'n sniff stickers still stuck to the bedpost. I could actually feel my pubic hair retracting back into my body. (. . .)

The only job left in all of Springfield, Virginia, was this one my mom found on back of the Springfield Excite Community Magazine—she cut it out really neatly and left it on the table. Takeout Taxi. "Work in a new friendly growing bursting business." I called.

(As employer.) "Ok Ok OK I'm Steve I am the founder and president of Takeout Taxi. How old are you? Can you drive. Can you write. Are you a Satanist. Are you a convict. Alrighty congratulations, welcome aboard, you'll be working as a Takeout Taxi technical assistant. Training will begin on

Thursday at eight o'clock in the Petland Discount Plaza. I'll see you there, I'll call you back if there are any changes," and I was like "Oh no, I will call YOU to discuss it further, thank YOU for your time and consideration."

I was psyched because I remembered Mrs. Fields got started with one cookie and a spatula and look at her.

Tammy

Steven Schutzman

Play
70s
Seriocomic

Tammy, a vigorous Jewish man in his seventies, is in a swim-
ming pool with his son who several hours before, walked into
Tammy's apartment to find his father embracing his African-
American cleaning woman.

Her name is Elvira, Nathan, and she has been my cleaning
woman since from soon after your mother died. From Jamaica
she is and almost my age but with young skin and a beautiful
smile in her eyes. They don't age like we do but slower like
good wood does. *(Beat.)* One day a few months ago, before
anything started, I walk into my bedroom where Elvira is putting my clothes away and she has in fact her face in a shirt of
mine, smelling it. I see her at this and perhaps I know I have
caught her at something and perhaps I don't, but I hear my
voice say a question, "Clean?" it says to her and she says "No,
it smells of you, which is a very lovely smell to me, Sir." Can
you imagine me hearing those words? Because Elvira and I have
always gotten along very well, playing cards in the afternoons
sometimes, afternoons I looked forward to, like food to my
loneliness but it was never until that moment that I considered
her a woman. Then all of a sudden she is very much of a
woman to me and we lay down on the bed. She's a great grand-
mother already with strong legs that still have to work at her
age. And take the bus over. Can you imagine the strength? I
don't have it anymore but I make her laugh. To her I am the
funniest man left alive. Because I don't give a crap. I am who I
am and she is who she is.

Thane of Cawdor
Don Nigro

Play
40
Dramatic

John Campbell has married the troubled young heiress Muriel Cawdor to become Thane of Cawdor. She has recently discovered she was kidnapped as a child by the Campbells so they could get their hands on her fortune. She has loved her husband, but she now feels betrayed by him. This is John defending himself to his wife.

Listen to me. These matters are not things which either you or I could have changed. Neither one of us made this. These are brutal times in a brutal place. Most die young. Those who survive live in poverty and ignorance and fear. This castle, this drafty old monstrosity, is what protects you from all that, as Inverary protected you, as my father protected you, as I protect you. It is true that I am capable of violence. I must be so to survive in this time and place, and if I were not so, trust me, you would be raped and murdered before the end of the week by some sadistic lunatic or other. I am violent when I must be. But I have never been violent towards you, nor would I ever be. And however you came to be here, Muriel, the truth is, you are loved now, by me, in this place, at this time, you are very deeply loved. And if in your stubborn rage you allow yourself to deny the simple truth of that, then you throw away a very precious thing, and you have once more lost one who cherishes you.

This Wakeful Night
Rosary O'Neill

Play
30s
Dramatic

December, 1882. Albert Sampite is a wealthy planter with charm and devilish good looks. Albert speaks to Kate at the Chopin plantation in Cloutierville, Louisiana.

(*ALBERT draws coffee slowly to his lips. His voice is intimate and slow.*)

I'm happier about the divorce than I was about the marriage. What religion forbids divorce, if people are miserable and want to kill each other? We should torture our spouses for the Church? I've stayed married for two thousand years. Lived with a woman, blaming me for our dead children. She lost four out of six. You never get over it. You get used to it. I spent too much time denying, clawing my way to sanity. Gave up warmth and companionship. Became a cowboy on the range; bucking and fighting . . . I rationalized coldness till it felt right to me. I work fifteen-hour days. Retreat here at night.

I love my children, but I can't stay with her for them. Hour by hour a part of me dies.

I do without. The servants say when I leave, my wife hums and sings.

(*Looking out the window.*)

That tree is still asleep but you know the hope that it's going to grow. That's what I want, someone to grow with. I doubt I'll find that. I'm a loner. I walk the fields at night, watching things grow, things die. It's a rush of power to know you own the land and can face the cold wastes alone. (*Pause.*) But it's also nice to see the warm glow in your window.

Throw Pitchfork

Alexander Thomas

Play
20s-30s
Comic

Alex recalls happy days in the Big Apple.

My big brother Cleve was out of College and living in New York City. I moved down to room with him. He was going to be a brilliant, unique writer: James Baldwin, Tennessee Williams, Baudelaire, and Blake all rolled into one. I was going to be a famous and intense actor: Robert De Niro, James Earl Jones, Al Pacino, Marlon Brando all rolled into one. We had a funky little apartment on the Lower East Side of New York City. Sixth Street between Avenue C n' D. Bohemian, baby, Bohemian. Struggling, starving artists, we were very, very, creative. Every morning we woke up and consumed massive amounts of beer. Usually the icebox consisted of a half dozen eggs, some potatoes, a six-pack of Budweiser, my favorite, and couple of quarts of Colt 45, Cleve's favorite. We took turns serving as each other's personal valet. *(In a stuffy English butler voice:)*

"Good morning Master Cleve, for breakfast today we shall have scrambled eggs à la scrambled eggs, smothered with deep pan-fried potatoes along with your favorite elixir, Colt 45. Oh I do beg your pardon sir, we seem to be out of both eggs and potatoes as well. We do however have an ample supply of Budweiser and Colt 45. Oh well, breakfast is breakfast."

And then we would get drunk and have our usual big brother little brother chat.

'Tis Better

Clinton A. Johnston

Original Monologue
20+
Comic

. . . to give than receive.

You don't do that! You don't just give people gifts!

It's not Chanukah. It's not Christmas. It's not my anniversary. It's not Kwanzaa. It's not my birthday. *Then*, you give gifts. Those are "Gift Giving Days"!

Fine, you give me a gift. What am I supposed to do now, huh? Do I get you a gift? Do I get you a gift now just because you got me a gift? Do I get you the same type of gift? What if your gift is more expensive than mine? Does that mean I love you less? How do we keep track? How do we budget? All these worries are spared us, why? Because we are a civilized society! Because we have rules and tradition and ritual to make sure that the *fabric* of our interactions remains strong and sturdy! But that doesn't work for you, does it? No, you're too good for the bonds and ties that keep us together, you with your over-romanticized views of individualism and your warped confusion of nonconformity with sincerity. You, you self-righteous, peevish, anarchistic putz, you would just go your own way and everyone else be damned! Well, I will not have you bring your culture-smashing chaos into our relationship!

Tongues, Part 2
Heidi Decker

Play
45-65
Dramatic

Having negotiated a truce with the voices in his head, a schizo-phrenic discovers silence is worse. Agitated, he speaks very quickly at first.

No, I'm not OK it's not OK everything is not going to be OK! Do you get that? Just stop saying it stop fucking saying that everything is going to be OK! You don't know.

I know you want to make me feel better but that's not the way to do it. You standing there lying to me only makes me feel worse . . . more alone. I was all wrong. An ultimatum. Was wrong. Stupid. I used to think that if they would just be quiet, just shut up for five damn minutes and let me think . . . let me breathe . . . but then they did. They were quiet. One day they just stopped. There was quiet inside my head. Like a cool breeze.

And you'd think it would be peaceful . . . serene, maybe. After all this time of wanting that so much, you'd think that would be like heaven. But the thing is, just because they were quiet doesn't mean they weren't still there. I could still feel them . . . only now they were no longer speaking to me. Or around me. Which was just so much worse.

I learned that silent disapproval is actually worse than being yelled at all the time.

Topdog/Underdog
Suzan-Lori Parks

Play
Late 20s
Dramatic

Lincoln and Booth, brothers and roommates, barely scrape out a living in demeaning circumstances. Their mother left them when they were small. Booth remembers her last words.

You know what Mom told me when she was packing to leave? You was at school motherfucker you was at school. You got up that morning and sat down in yr regular place and read the cereal box while Dad read the sports section and Mom brought you yr dick toast and then you got on the damn school bus cause you didnt have the sense to do nothing else you was so into yr own shit that you didn't have the sense to feel nothing else going on. I had the sense to go back cause I was feeling something going on man, I was feeling something changing. So I— (. . .)

    She was putting her stuff in bags. She had all them nice suitcases but she was putting her stuff in bags. (*Rest.*) Packing up her shit. She told me to look out for you. I told her I was the little brother and the big brother should look out after the little brother. She just said it again. That I should look out for you. Yeah. So who gonna look out for me.

Topdog/Underdog
Suzan-Lori Parks

Play
Late 20s
Seriocomic

Lincoln, holding take-out food, dispenses advice to his ironically named brother, Booth.

You gonna call yrself something african? That be cool. Only pick something that's easy to spell and pronounce, man, cause you know, some of them african names, I mean, OK, Im down with the power to the people thing, but, no ones gonna hire you if they cant say yr name. And some of them fellas who got they african names, no one can say they names and they cant say they names neither. I mean, you don't want yr new handle to obstruct yr employment possibilities. (. . .)

"Shango" would be a good name.

The name of the thunder god. If you aint decided already Im just throwing it in the pot. I brought chinese.

Topdog/Underdog
Suzan-Lori Parks

Play
Late 20s
Dramatic

Lincoln and Booth, brothers, roommates, and rivals, barely scrape together a living in demeaning circumstances. Booth had high hopes for a committed relationship with Grace, who stood him up the night before.

I popped her. (. . .)

Grace. I popped her. Grace. (*Rest.*) Who thuh fuck she think she is doing me like she done? Telling me I don't got nothing going on. I showed her what I got going on. Popped her good. Twice. Three times. Whatever. (*Rest.*) She ain't dead. (*Rest.*) She weren't wearing my ring I gived her. Said it was too small. Fuck that. Said it hurt her. Fuck that. Said she was into bigger things. *Fuck* that. She's alive not to worry, she ain't going out that easy she's alive she's she's—. (. .) Dead.

The Trophy Room
Hilly Hicks, Jr.

Play
20s
Dramatic

Allen has insight as to why his brother, Lewis wants to be a Marine.

I feel Kenneth kicking into my side. And I'm holding on to his leg. Trying to keep it from coming so hard. But I can't hold on tight enough, so the kicks keep coming harder and harder. Then I look back around for Lewis, and he isn't there. I'm still holding Kenneth's leg, but the kicking stops. And then there's Lewis, on the other side of me now, pushing Kenneth in the chest. Kenneth trips over me and falls. But Lewis picks him up and pushes him again. He pushes him into his brother and says something to them, but I can't hear it. Lewis hasn't so much as scratched them. But whatever he's doing, it's enough. And they're staring us down. Lewis helps me up, and we're walking away. I think my rib's broken, but I'm just walking like nothing happened. Now, I'm a little bit afraid they're gonna come running up behind us. But Lewis is just walking, eyes straight ahead. So I am, too. *(Beat.)* We haven't said a word to each other the whole way home. But just before we get to your lot, Pop. He turns to me and says, "I'm gonna be a Marine, Allen. What do you think about that?" I just said, "Marines are lucky."

The Trophy Room
Hilly Hicks, Jr.

Play
55
Dramatic

Joel tells his son the moment he "lost" his older son, Lewis, a once promising young student who got his girlfriend pregnant.

I was never the kind of father to hit his children. But that was something— I couldn't let that go. We had goals, me and him. I didn't want him straying anymore. So I took off my belt and . . . Ten times I hit him. And he gritted his teeth, but that didn't keep him from crying. But he was crying like a whisper. Couldn't hardly hear him . . . He was pleading with me not to tell the family. He didn't want his brother and sister to know what he'd done. I told him I wasn't gonna say anything to you, but he was gonna have to do some things for me. He had to get his concentration back. He was gonna have to take some more classes. Get ready for college. He was gonna put more hours in at his job, so he could take care of a family. Didn't matter, though. Lisette disappeared and had her baby somewhere else. He never saw her again. And he was glad. A year or so later she started trying to call him up on the phone. I asked her about that baby. My grandchild. It wasn't even born alive. *(Long pause.)* But after that night in the backyard . . . I lost him. He was going all out of control and I couldn't stop him . . .

The Trophy Room
Hilly Hicks, Jr.

Play
55
Dramatic

*Joel's grief and anger over his son's death finds release as he
buries his son's high school trophies.*

I warned you . . . I warned you again and again. I told you
every choice you make comes with consequences! This is the
price you paid! *(Beat.)* You forgot you had a family! You forgot
about us! You dragged us all onto that battlefield! Out there
pretending to be a hero. You ain't a hero. You're just a runny-
nose little brat! No respect for me! For your mother! For yourself! Just a brat . . . ! Scared. Lazy . . . Look how you ended
up— Look— Just look . . . what you did to yourself . . . ! Look
what you did to your family!
    *(JOEL pauses, unwelcome emotions overwhelming him. He
wipes his face and begins to throw the trophies into the hole.)*
    You think these trophies make you a hero? They make you
nothing . . . You're working on Allen, now. I see that! You're
trying to do it again! But I'm not gonna let you . . . You're not
gonna touch him . . . I've been through this before with you.
But that was the last time. You are not gonna do this again!
    *(He begins to refill the hole with dirt, covering the trophies.
His face is becoming stained with tears, which reflect the moonlight and fall into the dirt.)*
    Not gonna do that to this family twice. If you can forget
about us, we can forget about you!

Two Rooms
Lee Blessing

Play
30s
Dramatic

*Michael, an American educator in Beirut, has been taken
hostage. Alone, blindfolded, and handcuffed, he remembers his
colleague, also kidnapped.*

Mathison had a gun. Under his jacket. A little automatic pistol
or something—I'd never seen it before. Silver. I remember it
gleamed in the sunlight when he pulled it out. It was just as
they were forcing us both into the car—just as he put one hand
on the roof of the car. He was right in front of me, there was
nowhere I could go. And suddenly this shining little fantasy pistol appeared. Can you imagine? I taught for two years with the
guy and never knew he carried it. As though that was supposed
to save us. As though that pitiful gun—that absurd, miniscule
tribute to one man's utter lack of realism . . . I mean, he had to
know what the world can do—if it just *feels* like it—to a man.
To any man. And to carry a gun? The size of a cigarette case?
In Beirut? *(He starts to laugh, stops because it hurts.)* He didn't
even know what to do once he pulled it out. I think he really
believed all those kidnappers would take one look at this
mighty weapon of the West, drop their AK-47's and flee. "Run!
It's a trap! He's got a tiny gun!" *(Starts to laugh again, stops)*

Wedding Dance
Dominic Taylor

Play
20s-30s
Comic

Milton gets down.

Welcome to the Chateau Get Down, where your mission this evening is to get your groove on baby. See, out here when we grooving like we grooving, and you moving like you moving, it is the quintessential experience of experiences. The thought for the evening is happiness. The mood for the evening is love. And when you got them together, and you flip the script, you know you got—Love and Happiness, make you wanna do wrong do right. Make you wanna come home early, wanna make you stay out all night long.

Makes you wanna party deep. Makes you want to be not just knee deep, but totally deep. You hear what I'm saying? Make you wanna sing like, hey, hey!!! Make you get your Boogie on the Woogie, or as the old folks used to say, just get on the good foot!

Werthheimer Is Dead/
Long Live Werthheimer
Steven Schutzman

Play
30
Comic

*Josh is a creative guy in a nowhere job and can't seem to break
out of his rut. He is speaking to Jean, whom he has loved since
childhood.*

I have this dream where I'm a stand-up comic. I'm supposed to
go on in an hour and I feel great about it, going to knock 'em
dead. But something's nagging at me, slightly, very slightly. Oh
yeah, I remember: I better get my material together. But then I
remember I don't really have any material so I better work
some up before I go on. Though I'm really not worried since I
have a whole hour. Time passes, time I spend enjoyably thinking about how great I'm going be on stage. Then it's a half hour
before I'm supposed to go on and I remember again, no material, better do something about the material though I still have a
whole half hour. Not to worry. I'll be great. And so on and so
forth, more time passing, more enjoyable thinking, fifteen minutes to go, a little bit worried now, but thinking: I'm a stand-up
comic, I must have lots of great material. It'll come to me.
Going to be great. Be a big star. One minute to go, folded into
the folds of the curtains. Holy shit! What am I doing? Too late
to work up anything now. All I want is the enjoyable thinking,
so I enjoyably think some more about how great I'm going to
be. Oh it's wonderful. It'll be wonderful. Seven seconds to go,
six, five, four, three, two, one and you have to understand that

this last one second takes forever to pass, everything slowed down, folded in the folds of the curtains. And in that last eternal second I decide not to be a comedian on stage but to turn myself into a bear and scare the shit out of everybody.

What You Pawn I Will Redeem

Sherman Alexie

Short Story
Late 20s
Dramatic

The narrator, a homeless Native American, introduces himself.

I'm a Spokane Indian boy, an interior Salish, and my people have lived within a hundred-mile radius of Spokane, Washington, for at least ten thousand years. I grew up in Spokane, moved to Seattle twenty-three years ago for college, flunked out after two semesters, worked various blue and bluer-collar jobs, married two or three times, fathered two or three kids, and then went crazy. Of course, crazy is not the official definition of my mental problem, but I don't think asocial disorder fits it, either, because that makes me sound like I'm a serial killer or something. I've never hurt another human being, or, at least, not physically. I've broken a few hearts in my time, but we've all done that, so I'm nothing special in that regard. I'm a boring heartbreaker, too. I never dated or married more than one woman at a time. I didn't break hearts into pieces overnight. I broke them slowly and carefully. And I didn't set any land-speed records running out the door. Piece by piece, I disappeared. I've been disappearing ever since.

Where Girls Grow Strong:
An Archie Levine Piece

Todd Ristau

Original Monologue
40+
Seriocomic

Author's note: "To be performed as an angry rant in the style of Lewis Black or Andy Rooney after being kept in a cage for a week fed only Mexican food and tequila."

Hey. I'm Archie Levine, and *this* is what *I* think.

Some of George Bush's Base down in Waco, Texas, want you to *abstain* from buying and eating Girl Scout Cookies.

The guy must have a point, because *only Democrats* politicize issues for political gain. I looked into his argument against these little girls in their deceptively innocent paramilitary green uniforms, their sweetly disarming smiles and guise of wholesome innocence. I looked and what I saw *made me want to puke.*

John Pisciotta, director of Pro-Life Waco and an associate professor of economics at Baylor University, has exposed these evil little bitches for what they are. Rabid promoters of sexual perversity through their cozy relationship with Planned Parenthood's annual sex education seminars.

That's right. They come on all innocent, but they're *in bed* with the same smut peddlers and baby killers who are ruining this country. "Reproductive freedom." *That's code, man!* (. . .)

It all starts with the cookies. When one of these six-year-old left-wing liberal marriage-destroying America-hating terrorists comes ringing your door bell, call Tom Ridge. Not one penny of your hard-earned cookie money ought to go toward this anti-family abortion-on-demand condom-club member. (. . .)

Strike a blow against "reproductive freedom" and slam the door in the face of a Girl Scout today. Strike a blow for family values and the core beliefs that make this nation great. Strike a Girl Scout.

Winner of the National Book Award

Jincy Willett

Novel
Late 30s
Dramatic

Frank confesses to Dorcas he may be responsible for her sister's promiscuity.

We were all out on the ice and drunk as skunks. (. . .) We had just been carousing, you know, whooping it up and full of . . . well, booze, obviously, but also joy. Real joy. I was never that happy again. And your sister stayed with us, like a mascot. She was fun. (. . .) And then, I don't know, we were horsing around on the ice, and then she was standing there, and we are all standing around her in a circle, watching.

(. . .) She said, "What happens now?" Her voice wasn't scared. We didn't say anything. We didn't know! She said, "What do you want me to do?" And somebody said, "Take off your sweater." *I* said it. And she did. And someone else told her what to take off next, and so on. (. . .) We didn't look at each other, or move.

(. . .) She danced. She didn't dance like a stripper or a whore. (. . .) She raised her arms and turned, around and around, (. . .) but not being obscene, just showing. I have never in my life seen anyone as happy as she was then.

All the guys threw their jackets down. She thought they were giving her a bigger dance floor. She thought that this was what we wanted. To watch her dance.

(. . .) She didn't understand that she couldn't stop it.

The Worrying

Paul Monette

Poem
40s+
Dramatic

The stress and emotions surrounding the care of a terminally ill lover.

[*The worrying*] ate me alive day and night these land mines
all over like the toy bombs dropped on the
Afghans little Bozo jack-in-the-boxes
that blow your hands off three AM I'd go
around the house with a rag of ammonia
wiping wiping crazed as a housewife on *Let's
Make a Deal* the deal being PLEASE DON'T MAKE
HIM SICK AGAIN faucets doorknobs the phone
every lethal thing a person grips and leaves
his prints on scrubbed my hands till my fingers
cracked washed apples ten times ten no salad but
iceberg and shuck the outer two-thirds someone
we knew was brain dead from sushi so stick
to meat loaf creamed corn spuds whatever we
could cook to death DO NOT USE THE D WORD
EVEN IN JEST when you started craving deli
I heaved a sigh because salami was so de-
germed with its lovely nitrites to hell with
cholesterol that's for people way way over
the hill or up the hill not us in the vale
of borrowed time

You Will Fall in Love With Me

Adam Hahn

Original Monologue
20s
Comic

Standing in front of a mirror, Loverboy prepares for a date by practicing his powers of suggestion.

You will fall in love with me.

Up to this point, our relationship has been ambiguous, and perhaps you have been unsure how to feel about me.

You will fall in love with me.

We share a connection, you and I. You agreed to this date tonight because you sense this. You cannot resist me.

Tonight, I will be warm, and charming, and adorable. I will take you to see *The Hours*, and later, to Village Inn.

You will fall in love with me.

I will see you naked. You will see me naked, and we will be naked together. Neither of us will laugh.

You and I will make love. Not tonight, because you are not a slut, and I do not date sluts. Perhaps next weekend.

You will fall in love with me.

You will be unlike all other girls I have dated. After tonight's date, you will not avoid me. You will not fall out of love with me. You will not decide you are more in love with your ex-boyfriend. You will not tell me I am too "creepy" or "obsessive." You will enjoy giving and receiving oral sex.

You will fall in love with me.

MONOLOGUES BY AGE

20s-30s

30+

40s-50s

50s

50+

60+

MONOLOGUES BY TONE

Seriocomic Monologues

MONOLOGUES BY VOICE

Circle A. © 2005 by Cathy Camper. Reprinted by permission of the author.

Cities of the Mountain. © 1996 by Jim Cowen. Reprinted by permission of the author.

Closure (from *Pure Drivel*). © 1998 by Steve Martin. Reprinted by permission of

International Creative Management, 40 W. 57th St., New York, NY 10019.

Coercion. © 2004 by Katie Leo. Reprinted by permission of the author.

Concerned Catholics. © 2002 by Barbara Lhota and Janet Milstein. Reprinted by permission of the authors.

Confessions of a Recovering Teenager. © 2005 by Jonathan Dorf. Reprinted by permission of the author.

Crush Everlasting. © 2003 by Dave Ulrich. Reprinted by permission of the author.

The Curious Incident of the Dog in the Night-Time. © 2003 by Mark Haddon. Reprinted by permission of Doubleday, a division of Random House, Inc., 1745 Broadway, New York, NY 10019.

Curse of the Starving Class. © 1976, 2004 by Sam Shepard. Reprinted by permission of. Bantam Books, a division of Random House, Inc., 1745 Broadway, New York, NY 10019. The entire text has been published in a trade edition by Bantam (*Seven Plays by Sam Shepard*), and in an acting edition by Dramatists Play Service, which also handles performance rights (see contact information below).

Cuthbert's Last Stand. © 2001 by Andrew Biss. Reprinted by permission of the author.

Daddy Garbage (from *The Stories of John Edgar Wideman*). ©1981, 1992 by John Edgar Wideman. Reprinted by permission of Pantheon Books, A division of Random House, Inc., 1745 Broadway, New York, NY 10019.

Daddy's Home. © 2001 by Henry W. Kimmel. Reprinted by permission of the author.

Dangerous Dave and the Whalers. © 2005 by Lawrence Krauser. Reprinted by permission of the author.

Dear Chuck. © 2002 by Jonathan Dorf. Reprinted by permission of Eldridge Publishing, Box 14367, Tallahassee, FL 32317, which has published the entire text in an acting edition and which also handles performance rights.

Irene Ziegler Aston is an actor and writer in Richmond, Virginia. Her play, *Rules of the Lake,* won the Mary Roberts Rinehart award. Irene narrated the award-winning documentary film, *In the Face of Evil: Ronald Reagan's War in Word and Deed.* She is completing a novel.

John Capecci is a communications consultant and writer based in Minneapolis. He holds a Ph.D. in Performance Studies and has taught communication performance methods for over fifteen years.